THE LABOURS

OF

HERCULES

BOOKS BY ALICE A. BAILEY

Initiation, Human and Solar
Letters on Occult Meditation
The Consciousness of the Atom
A Treatise on Cosmic Fire
The Light of the Soul
The Soul and its Mechanism
From Intellect to Intuition
A Treatise on White Magic
From Bethlehem to Calvary
Discipleship in the New Age–Vol. I
Discipleship in the New Age–Vol. II
Problems of Humanity
The Reappearance of the Christ
The Destiny of the Nations
Glamour: A World Problem
Telepathy and the Etheric Vehicle
The Unfinished Autobiography
Education in the New Age
The Externalisation of the Hierarchy
A Treatise on the Seven Rays:
Vol. I–Esoteric Psychology
Vol. II–Esoteric Psychology
Vol. III–Esoteric Astrology
Vol. IV–Esoteric Healing
Vol. V–The Rays and the Initiations

THE LABOURS OF HERCULES

An Astrological Interpretation

by

ALICE A. BAILEY

LUCIS PUBLISHING COMPANY
New York

LUCIS PRESS LIMITED
London

This book is a reprint of articles that first appeared in The BEACON magazine between February 1957 and August 1958.

The publication of this book is financed by the Tibetan Book Fund which is established for the perpetuation of the teachings of the Tibetan and Alice A. Bailey.

This Fund is controlled by the Lucis Trust, a tax-exempt, religious, educational corporation.

The Lucis Publishing Companies are non-profit organisations owned by the Lucis Trust. No royalties are paid on this book.

This book has been translated into Danish, Dutch, French, German, Greek, Italian, Portuguese, Russian, Spanish. Translation into other languages is proceeding.

LUCIS PUBLISHING COMPANY
120 Wall Street
New York, NY 10005

LUCIS PRESS LIMITED
Suite 54
3 Whitehall Court
London SW1A 2EF

www.lucistrust.org

MANUFACTURED IN THE UNITED STATES OF AMERICA

THE GREAT INVOCATION

From the point of Light within the Mind of God
Let light stream forth into the minds of men.
Let Light descend on Earth.

From the point of Love within the Heart of God
Let love stream forth into the hearts of men.
May Christ return to Earth.

From the centre where the Will of God is known
Let purpose guide the little wills of men—
The purpose which the Masters know and serve.

From the centre which we call the race of men
Let the Plan of Love and Light work out.
And may it seal the door where evil dwells.

Let Light and Love and Power restore the Plan on Earth.

"The above Invocation or Prayer does not belong to any person or group but to all Humanity. The beauty and the strength of this Invocation lies in its simplicity, and in its expression of certain central truths which all men, innately and normally, accept—the truth of the existence of a basic Intelligence to Whom we vaguely give the name of God; the truth that behind all outer seeming, the motivating power of the universe is Love; the truth that a great Individuality came to earth, called by Christians, the Christ, and embodied that love so that we could understand; the truth that both love and intelligence are effects of what is called the Will of God; and finally the self-evident truth that only through *humanity* itself can the Divine Plan work out."

ALICE A. BAILEY.

TABLE OF CONTENTS

THE ZODIAC

The Presiding One looked forth upon the sons of men, who are the Sons of God. He saw their light and where they stood upon the *Way* which leads back to the Heart of God. The *Way* sweeps in a circle through the twelve great Gates, and, cycle after cycle, the Gates are opened and the Gates are shut. The Sons of God, who are the sons of men, march on.

Dim is the light at first. Selfish the trend of human aspiration, and dark the deeds resultant. Slowly men learn and, in learning, pass between the pillars of the Gates time and again. Dull is the understanding but in the Halls of Discipline, found in each section of the circle's cosmic sweep, the truth is slowly grasped; the needed lesson learnt; the nature purified and taught until the Cross is seen – that fixed and waiting Cross which crucifies the sons of men, stretched out on the Crosses of those who serve and save.

From out the mass of men, one man stood forth in ancient days and caught the great presiding Elder's watching eye, he who eternally presides within the Council Chamber of the Lord. He turned to one who stood, close at his hand, and said: "Who is that soul upon the *Way* of life, whose light can now be dimly seen?"

Quickly the answer came: "That is the soul who, on the *Way* of life, experiences and seeks the clear light which shines from the High Place".

"Let him proceed upon his way, but watch his steps".

The swiftly passing aeons ran their course. The great wheel turned and, turning, brought the seeking soul upon the *Way*. Later, there came a day when the Presiding One, within the Council Chamber of the Lord, again drew to the circle of his radiant life the seeking soul.

"Whose is this soul upon the *Way* of high endeavour whose radiance dimly shineth forth?" Came the reply: "A soul who seeks the light of understanding, a struggling soul".

"Tell him from me to return the other way and then to travel round the circle. Then will he find the object of his search. Watch o'er his steps and, when he has an understanding heart, an eager mind and skilful hand, bring him to me."

Again the centuries passed. The great wheel turned and, in turning, carried all the sons of men, who are the Sons of God, upon their way. And as these centuries passed, a group of men emerged who slowly turned the other way. They found the *Way*. They passed the Gates and struggled towards the mountain top, and towards the place of death and sacrifice. The watching Teacher saw a man emerge from out this crowd, mount the fixed Cross, demanding deeds to do, service to render unto God and man, and willingness to travel the *Way* to God. He stood before the great Presiding One who works within the Council Chamber of the Lord and heard a word go forth:

"Obey the Teacher on the Way. Prepare for the last tests. Pass through each Gate and in the sphere which they reveal and guard, perform the labour which befits their sphere. Learn thus the lesson and begin with love to serve the men of earth". Then to the Teacher went the final word: "Prepare the candidate. Give him his labours to perform and place his name upon the tablets of the living *Way*".

THE TIBETAN.

FOREWORD: THE PURPOSE OF THIS STUDY

The intense interest evinced at this time in the subject of the spiritual life is in itself the warrant for such a study as this series of articles purposes. In defiance of the fact that academic and theological religion has no longer its ancient appeal and in spite of the revolt against organised religion, the urge towards spiritual realities has never been so keen as now. The day of empirical experience on a large scale is now with us, and men and women everywhere are refusing any longer to believe and blindly accept, because they are determined to know. Acceptance of imposed dogmas is now giving place to experiment, and a divine self-determination, based on a realised unity with the Life in which we live and move and have our being, is taking the place of credulity and superstition.

The problem of every teacher today is to discover new ways in which to express the old truths, and so present the ancient formulas for spiritual development that they will acquire new and vivid life. In both hemispheres there have been many books written on the subject of the Path of Discipleship, the Path of Holiness, and the Path of Illumination. The restatement of the problems of that universal Path and of its inherent difficulties is not warranted unless the application can be modern and practical. It must indicate the inclusiveness of the goal, once those problems have been surmounted, and must avoid the tiresome reiteration of that basic rule of life, which has been expressed in the two words: "Be good". Again and again we have been told that we must overcome the lure of the world, the flesh and the devil. There has been built up in the mind of the western aspirant a feeling that the Path is necessarily one of misery, of self-abnegation and of endless distress. His attitude is one of active endurance until such time as he mysteriously and miraculously breaks through into a world of peace and plenty, wherein all troubles come to an end, the flesh ceases to annoy, and the devil comes to an untimely end. And this as the reward of a meek submission to the will of an inscrutable creator.

There is, however, dawning on the human consciousness, a growing realisation of innate divinity and that man is in very truth made in the image of God, and one in nature with his Father in Heaven. The idea of purpose and of plan is being grasped, and the entire attitude of the aspirant towards life is rapidly changing. Surely it should now be possible to gain such a synthetic picture of the progress of the soul from ignorance to wisdom, from material desire to spiritual achievement that the end may be visioned from the beginning and intelligent co-operation with soul purpose take the place of blind endeavour? When this comes about, the pilgrim can proceed upon his way with his face turned towards the light, and irradiated with joy.

The story of the dramatic experiences of that great and ancient Son of God, Hercules or Herakles, will be found to give us just such a synthetic picture. It leaves untouched no phase in the life of the aspirant and yet links him up with cosmic enterprise. Its theme will be found to be so inclusive that all of us, struggling in our present modern life, can make application to ourselves of the tests and trials, the failures and achievements of this heroic Figure, who strove, centuries ago, towards the same goal as we do. Through a reading of his story, fresh interest may be evoked in the mind of the bewildered aspirant, and such a picture painted of universal sequential development and destiny that he will go forward with fresh courage.

We shall trace the story of Hercules and endeavour to show how he, in his twelve labours, played the part of the aspirant upon the Path of Discipleship. On it, he undertook certain tasks, symbolic in nature, and passed through certain episodes and events which portray for all time the nature of the training and attainments which characterise the man who is nearing liberation. He stands for the incarnated, yet not perfected, Son of

God, who definitely takes the lower nature in hand and willingly subjects it to the discipline which will eventually produce the emergence of divinity. Out of an erring but sincerely earnest human being, intelligently aware of the work to be accomplished, a World Saviour is formed.

Two great and dramatic stories have been held constantly before the eyes of men down the ages. In the twelve labours of Hercules, that Path of Discipleship is depicted, and his experiences preparatory to the great concluding cycle of Initiation meet with a ready response from every aspiring man. In the life and work of Jesus the Christ, that radiant and perfected Son of God, who "has entered for us within the veil, leaving us an example that we should follow his steps", we have portrayed the five stages of the Path of Initiation, which are the climaxing episodes for which the twelve labours have prepared the disciple.

The oracle has spoken, and down the ages the word has sounded forth: Man, know thyself. This knowledge is the outstanding attainment upon the Path of Discipleship, and the reward of all the work done by Hercules.

The Nature of Discipleship

It might be of value here if we considered briefly the nature of discipleship. It is a word in constant use among aspirants in Christian lands, as in the oriental religions. Discipleship could be defined as the final stage of the path of evolution, and as that period in a man's experience in which he is definitely self-conscious. It is the stage in which he knowingly pledges himself to impose the will of the soul (which is essentially the will of God) upon the lower nature. Upon this path he submits himself to a forcing process, so that the flower of the soul can unfold more quickly. The inevitability of human perfection underlies his willingness to make the attempt to tread the path. This perfection can be attained in two ways. It can be the result of slow and steady evolutionary growth, carried forward under nature's laws, cycle after cycle, until gradually the hidden God can be seen in man and in the universe. Or, it can be the result of systematised application and discipline on the part of the aspirant, producing a more rapid unfoldment of the power and life of the soul.

In one analysis of discipleship, it has been defined as "a psychic resolvent, which eats away all dross and leaves only the pure gold behind". It is a process of refining, of sublimation and of transmutation, carried steadily forward until at length the Mount of Transfiguration and of Illumination is attained. The hidden mysteries and the forces, latent in human beings, need to be discovered and require to be utilised in a divine manner and in line with divine purpose, intelligently apprehended. When they have thus been utilised, the disciple finds himself en rapport with the universal and similar divine energies and powers, underlying the operations of the natural world. Thus he becomes a worker under the plan of evolution and a co-operator with that great "cloud of witnesses", who through the power of their onlooking, and the result of their attainment, constitute the Thrones, Principalities and Powers through the medium of which the one Life guides all creation onward to a glorious consummation.

Such is the goal towards which Hercules worked, and such is the goal before humanity as a whole, whose ultimate group achievement will be brought about by the many individual perfections.

Astrological Connotations

A secondary object of this study is to present an aspect of astrology which will differ from that usually expressed. We shall trace the story of Hercules as he passed through the twelve signs of the zodiac. In each sign he expressed its characteristics, and in each sign, he achieved some fresh knowledge of himself, and through that knowledge demonstrated the power of the sign and acquired the gifts which the sign conferred. In each of the signs we shall find him surmounting his natural tendencies, controlling and governing his destiny, and demonstrating the fact that the stars incline, but do not control.

The form of astrology which will, I believe, in time supersede the ordinary kind, dealing with horoscopes, is that synthetic presentation of cosmic happenings which have their reflection in our planetary life, in the life of humanity as a whole, and in the life of the individual, who is ever the microcosm of the macrocosm. This type of astrology confines its attention primarily to the unfolding of the plan of the ages; this, history reveals in a small way as far as humanity is concerned, and a larger study of the times and seasons may bring to us a wider understanding of God's purposes. There is an immense past behind humanity; aeons and aeons have come and gone; the wheel of existence turns continuously, and ever the scroll of life unrolls, and we are carried forward on the impetus of a returning force towards a newer aspect of the goal, and a wider vision and realisation. Concentration upon the personal horoscope and the intense interest evinced by individuals in their own petty affairs may be natural and normal, but it is nevertheless myopic. The consciousness that we are integral parts of a greater Whole, and that knowledge of the divine sumtotal can alone reveal the vaster purpose. These are the ideas that must eventually supersede our personal concentrations. Our small life histories must disappear in the larger picture. Hercules astrologically enacted the life history of every aspirant, and demonstrated the part which the unit must play in the eternal Enterprise.

A great eastern Teacher has expressed in connection with the zodiac and astrology this suggestive thought:

"That astrology is a science and a coming science is true. That astrology in its highest aspect and its true interpretation will eventually enable man to focus his understanding and to function rightly is equally true. That in the revelations that astrology will make in time to come will be found the secret of the true co-ordination between soul and form is also correct. But that astrology has not yet been discovered. Too much is overlooked and too little known to make astrology the exact science that many claim it to be. The claim will be fulfilled at some future date, but the time is not yet.

"Astrology as now practised is doomed to break down, owing to the rapidity with which souls are controlling their personalities. The casting of the horoscope of the soul will not be based on our three dimensional knowledge, for the laws of time and space have no hold over the soul".

(*Esoteric Astrology*).

We will therefore in this study deal with an astrology which will be non-mathematical and which will have no relation to the casting of horoscopes. It will concern itself with the twelve types of energy by means of which consciousness of the divine Reality is brought about through the medium of form. In no distant heaven and in no subjective state did Hercules arrive at this knowledge. In the physical body, handicapped and limited by the tendencies conferred on him by the sign in which he performed the labour, he attained understanding of his own essential divinity. Through the overcoming of form and the subjugation of matter, a picture is given us of an unfolding divine self-realisation. In the study therefore of Hercules the disciple, and of Christ, the World Saviour, we have an entire pictorial presentation of the final stages of unfoldment which lie ahead of all of us. The five great Initiations as portrayed for us in the history of Jesus the Christ are not dealt with here, but form the subject of another book. (*From Bethlehem to Calvary*)

As we study the story of Hercules and go with him through his twelve labours, passing around the great zodiac of the heavens, we will approach it from two angles: that of the individual aspirant and that of humanity as a whole. It is now possible to regard the human family as having reached, practically *en masse,* the stage of the aspirant, the stage of the intelligent seeker, the stage of the man who, having developed his mind and co-ordinated his abilities, mental, emotional and physical, has exhausted the interests of the phenomenal world, and is looking for a way out into a wider realm of awareness, and into a more sure sphere of undertakings. This stage has always been expressed by the advanced individuals down the ages, but never before has the human race itself been in this condition. Herein lies the wonder of past achievement, and herein lies the hour of present opportunity.

The World Disciple Today

The tests to which Hercules willingly subjected himself and the labours into which he sometimes thoughtlessly rushed are those which are possible to many thousands now. It will become apparent also how curiously applicable to modern conditions are the various details of the dramatic and oft-times amusing story of his efforts upon the path of ascension. Each one of us is an embryo Hercules, and each one of us faces the identical labours; each of us has the same goal to achieve and the same circle of the zodiac to encompass. The work to be done has for its prime objective the elimination of all fear and the control of the natural forces of the human nature. These Hercules has to face in every possible combination before he climbs the mount of initiation in Capricorn and becomes the server of humanity.

Competition and selfish objectives have to be completely changed and eliminated, and we shall find Hercules learning the lesson that to grasp anything for the separated self is no part of the mission of a son of God. He has to find himself as an individual, only to discover that individualism must be sacrificed intelligently to the good of the group. He discovers likewise that personal greed has no place in the life of the aspirant who is seeking liberation from the ever recurring cycle of existence and the constant crucifixion upon the cross of matter. The characteristics of the man immersed in form life and under the rule of matter are fear, individualism, competition and greed. These have to give place to spiritual confidence, co-operation, group awareness and selflessness. This is the lesson that Hercules brings to us, and this is the demonstration of the life of God which is being wrought out in the creative process, and which flowers forth more beautifully each time that the life of God makes its sweep around the zodiac which, the astronomers tell us, takes approximately twenty-five thousand years to accomplish.

This is the story of the cosmic Christ, crucified upon the Fixed Cross of the heavens; this is the story of the historical Christ, given us in the gospel story and enacted two thousand years ago in Palestine; this is the story of the individual Christ, crucified upon the cross of matter, and incarnated in each human being, God, incarnate in matter. This is the story of our solar system, the story of our planet, the story of the human being. Thus as we look at the starry heavens above, we have eternally pictured for us this great drama, which the story of Hercules elucidates in detail for the aspirant.

Key Thoughts

Four key thoughts can be given here which express the underlying purpose of the creative process and the objective of both the Cosmic Christ and of the individual aspirant. They give us the clue to the working out of the plan. Taken together they embody the entire story of the relationship of spirit and matter, of life and form, and of soul and body.

First: "Nature expresses invisible energies through visible forms". Back of the objective world of phenomena, human or solar, small or great, organic or inorganic, lies a subjective world of forces which is responsible for the outer form. Behind the outer material shell is to be found a vast empire of BEING, and it is into this world of living energies that both religion and science are now penetrating. Everything outer and tangible is a symbol of inner creative forces and it is this idea that underlies all symbology. A symbol is an outer and visible form of an inner and spiritual reality.

It is with this interplay of the outer form and the inner life that Hercules wrestles. He knew himself to be the form, the symbol, for the dominance of the lower material nature made its presence felt with the facility of age-long expression. At the same time he knew that his problem was to express spiritual being and energy. He had to know in fact and in experience that he was God, immanent in nature; that he was the Self in close relation to the Not-Self; he had to experiment with the law of cause and effect, and this from the standpoint of the initiator of the causes in order to produce intelligent effects. Through the twelve signs of the zodiac he passed, struggling to work subjectively and trying to reject the lure and the pull of the outer tangible form.

The second key thought can be expressed in the words: "The conception of a concealed Deity lies at the heart of all religions". This is the mystic realisation and the object of the search that humanity has carried on down the ages. The exponents of the world religions have embodied in their teaching one aspect of the search, accepting the fact of God as a basic premise, and with their heart's love and devotion and worship proving the reality of his Existence. The testimony of the mystics of all time and races is so vast that it now in itself constitutes a body of proven facts and cannot be gainsaid.

The scientific investigators have sought through a knowledge of the form to find truth, and have brought us to a position of wide knowledge and at the same time to a paralleling conception of our profound ignorance. We have learned much of the outer garment of God through physics, chemistry, biology and other sciences, but we have struggled into a realm where all appears to be hypothesis and inference. All that we surely know is that all forms are aspects of energy; that there is an interplay and an impact of energies upon our planet; that the planet is itself an energy unit composed of a multitude of energy units, and that man himself is likewise a composite bundle of forces and moving in a world of force. This is where science so wonderfully has led us, and this is where the astrologer, the occultist, the idealist and the mystic also meet and testify to a concealed Deity, to a living Being, to a Universal Mind, and to a central Energy.

In the unfolding drama of the heavens, in the conclusions of the scientific enquirer, in the mathematical computations of the astrologers, and in the testimony of the mystic, however, we can see a steadily emerging manifestation of this concealed divinity. Little by little, through the study of history, of philosophy and of comparative religion, we see the plan of that Deity becoming significantly apparent. In the passage of the sun through the twelve signs of the zodiac, we can see the marvellous organisation of the plan, the focusing of the energies and the growth of the tendency towards divinity. Now, at last, in the twentieth century, objective and subjective have become so closely blended and merged that it is almost impossible to say where one begins and another ends. The veil that hides the concealed Deity is wearing thin, and the work of those who have achieved knowledge, the programme of the Christ and of his Church, the plans of the hidden band of world workers, the Rishis and the occult Hierarchy of our planet, is now focussed upon leading humanity on to the Path of Discipleship, and training many of the more advanced so that they can become the knowers and initiates of the new age. Thus men will pass out of the Hall of Learning into the Hall of Wisdom, from the realm of the unreal to the Real, and from the outer darkness of phenomenal existence into the light that shines always in the kingdom of spirit.

The third key thought gives us a clue to the method. Down the ages the words have sounded forth: "I am he . . . who awakens the silent beholder". It has become apparent to seekers in all fields that within all forms there is an urge to intelligent expression, and a certain livingness which we call consciousness, and which in the human family takes the form of a self-awareness.

This self-awareness when truly developed, enables a man to discover that the concealed Deity in the universe is identical in nature, though vastly greater in degree and consciousness, with the concealed Deity within himself. Man then can become consciously the Onlooker, the Beholder, the Perceiver. He is no longer identified with the matter aspect, but is the One who uses it as a medium of expression.

When this stage is reached, the great labours start, and the warfare is consciously in progress. The man is torn in two directions. Habit entices him to identify himself with form. The new understanding impels him to identify himself with the soul. A reorientation then takes place, and a new and self-directed effort is initiated, which is portrayed for us in the story of Hercules, the Sun-God. The moment that the intellectual altitude has been achieved, the "silent Beholder" awakens into activity. Hercules starts upon his labours. The human being, hitherto swept along on the urge of the evolutionary tide, and governed by desire for experience and for material possession, comes under the control of the divine Indweller. He emerges as the aspirant, reverses himself, and begins to work through the twelve signs of the zodiac, only now working from Aries to Pisces via Taurus (anti-clockwise), instead of working in the ordinary human retrogressive fashion, from Aries to Taurus via Pisces (clockwise).

Finally, the changing focus of the life and the steady application to the twelve labours in the twelve signs enables the disciple to become the triumphant victor. Then he can comprehend the significance of the fourth key thought and can exclaim in unison with the Cosmic Deity: "Listen to this great secret. Although I am above birth and rebirth, or Law, being the Lord of all there is, for all emanateth from me, still do I will to appear in my own universe and am therefore born by my Power and Thought and Will". (*The Bhagavad Gita,* as compiled and adapted by YOGI RAMACHARAKA).

HERCULES THE DISCIPLE—THE MYTH

He stood before his Teacher. Dimly he understood that a crisis was upon him, leading to change of speech, of attitude and plan. The Teacher looked him o'er and liked him well.

"Your name?" he asked and waited for an answer.

"Herakles", the answer came, "or Hercules. They tell me that it means Hera's rare glory, the radiance and effulgence of the soul. What is the soul, O Teacher? Tell me truth".

"That soul of yours, you shall discover as you do your task, and find and use the nature which is yours. Who are your parents? Tell me this, my son".

"My father is divine. I know him not, except that, in myself, I know I am his son. My mother is an earthly one. I know her well and she has made me what you see. Likewise, O Teacher of my life, I am also one of twins. There is another one, like unto me. I also know him well, yet know him not. One is of earth, thus earthly; the other is a son of God".

"What of your training, Hercules, my son? What can you do and how have you been taught?"

"In all accomplishments I am proficient; I am well taught, well trained, well guided and well known. All books I know, all arts and sciences as well; the labours of the open field are known to me, besides the skill of those who can afford to travel and know men. I know myself as one who thinks, and feels and lives."

"One thing, O Teacher, I must tell to you and thus deceive you not. The fact is not so long ago I slew all those who taught me in the past. I killed my teachers, and in my search for liberty, I now stand free. I seek to know myself, within myself and through myself".

"My son, that was a deed of wisdom, and now you can stand

free. Proceed to labour now, remembering as you do, that at the final turning of the wheel will come the mystery of death. Forget this not. What is your age, my son?"

"I had turned eighteen summers when I slew the lion, and hence I wear its skin. Again at twenty-one, I met my bride. Today I stand before you trebly free–free from my early teachers, free from the fear of fear, and free indeed from all desire".

"Boast not, my son, but prove to me the nature of this freedom which you sense. Again in Leo, will you meet the lion. What will you do? Again in Gemini, the teachers whom you slew will cross your path. Have you indeed left them behind? What will you do? Again in Scorpio, will you wrestle with desire. Will you stand free, or will the serpent meet you with his wiles and pull you down to earth? What will you do? Prepare to prove your words and liberty. Boast not, my son, but prove to me your freedom and your deep desire to serve".

The Teacher sat in silence and Hercules withdrew and faced the first great Gate. Then the Presiding One, who sat within the Council Chamber of the Lord, spoke to the Teacher and bade him call the gods to witness the endeavour and start the new disciple on the *Way*. The Teacher called. The gods replied. They came and gave to Hercules their gifts and many words of sage advice, knowing the tasks ahead and the perils of the *Way*.

Minerva handed him a robe, woven by herself, a robe that fitted well, of beauty rare and fine. He put it on, with triumph and with pride; exulting in his youth. He had to prove himself.

A golden breastplate Vulcan forged for Hercules, to guard his heart, the source of life and strength. This golden gift was girded on, and, shielded thus, the new disciple felt secure. He had yet to prove his strength.

Neptune arrived with horses twain and handed them, in leash, to Hercules. Straight from the place of waters came they, of beauty rare and proven strength. And Hercules was pleased, for he had yet to prove his power to ride the horses twain.

With graceful speech and brilliant wit came Mercury, carrying a sword of rare design, which he proffered, in a silver sheath, to Hercules. He strapped it on the thigh of Hercules, bidding him keep it sharp and bright. "It must divide and cut", said Mercury, "and with precision and acquired skill must move". And Hercules, with joyous words, tendered his thanks. He had yet to prove his boasted skill.

With blaring trumpets and the rush of stamping feet the chariot of the Sun God flashed. Apollo came and with his light and charm cheered Hercules, giving him a bow, a bow of light. Through nine wide open Gates must the disciple pass before he had acquired sufficient skill to draw that bow. It took him all that time to prove himself the Archer. Yet when the gift was proffered, Hercules took it, confident of power, a power as yet unproven.

And thus he stood equipped. The gods stood round his Teacher, and watched his antics and his joy. He played before the gods, and showed his prowess, boasting of his strength. Suddenly he paused and pondered long; then gave the horses to a friend to hold, the sword to still another and the bow unto a third. Then, running, disappeared into the nearby wood.

The gods awaited his return, wondering and puzzled over his strange conduct. Back from the wood he came, bearing aloft a club of wood, cut from a stalwart living tree.

"This is mine own", he cried, "none gave it to me. This I can use with power. O gods, watch my high deeds".

And then, and only then, the Teacher said: "Go forth to labour".

THE TIBETAN.

Elaboration of the Myth

We come now to a consideration of Hercules himself. It is a most interesting story, and one that has been treated by many writers. Discussion as to the details of his life, and argument as to the sequence of events, are not any part of our objective. The various accounts differ in detail, according to the bias of the historian, and can be studied in the many classical histories and dictionaries. We will deal here only with the twelve famous labours, and of them we read:

"Hercules, by the will of Jupiter, was subjected to the power of Eurystheus, and obliged to obey him in every demand. He consulted the oracle of Apollo and was told that he must be subservient for twelve years to the will of Eurystheus, in compliance with the commands of Jupiter; and that, after he had achieved the most celebrated labours, he should be translated to the gods".

So he started off upon his career and, as the disciple under command of his soul, undertook the twelve labours, performing each of them in one of the zodiacal signs. He, therefore, represents every disciple who seeks to tread the path and demonstrate his control over the forces of his nature, and he likewise represents the point at which humanity now finds itself.

His early name was Alkeides, which was changed to Hercules after he had undergone a strange experience, and before he started forth upon his labours. The name Hercules was originally Herakles, which signifies "the glory of Hera". Hera represents Psyche, or the soul, so his name embodied his mission, which was to manifest forth in active work on the physical plane the glory and the power of his innate divinity.

One of the ancient scriptures of India says: "By mastery of the binding life comes radiance", and it was this mastery of the imprisoning form which was the glorious consummation of all the undertakings of Hercules. We are told that he had a divine father and an earthly mother and so, as with all sons of God, we find the same basic symbology emerging. They typify in their persons the essential duality of God in manifestation, of life in form, of soul in body, and of spirit and matter. This duality is the glory of humanity and also constitutes the problem which every human being has to solve. Father-Spirit and Mother-Matter meet together in man, and the work of the disciple is to withdraw himself from the bonds of the mother and thus respond to the love of the Father.

This duality is also brought out in the fact that he was one of twins. We read that one twin was born of an earthly father, and that the other was the son of Zeus. This is the great realisation that comes to every developed and self-aware human being. He finds himself conscious of two aspects which meet in his nature. There is the well developed and highly organised personality through which he habitually expresses himself (mental, emotional and physical), with all three parts co-ordinated into an integrated unit. Then there is the spiritual nature, with its impulses and intuitions, its constant pull towards things vital and divine, and the consequent inner warfare which grows out of this realised duality. Hercules was the disciple, living in a physical body, but capable at times, like St. Paul, of being "caught up to the third heaven", and having intercourse with divine beings. In this condition, he visioned the Plan, knew what he had to do and perceived the reality of the spiritual life.

There is also one interesting little fact in the story of his life which has a bearing on this same truth. Whilst still an infant, we are told that Hercules killed his twin. He was no longer a divided entity, no longer a duality, but soul and body formed one unity. This indicates always the stage of the disciple. He has made the at-one-ment and knows himself to be soul in body and not soul and body, and this realisation has now to colour all his actions. Whilst in the cradle, history relates, the lusty infant killed two serpents, again emphasising duality. In this act he forecast the future in which he demonstrated that the physical nature no longer controlled, but that he could strangle the serpent of matter and that the great illusion no longer had him imprisoned. He slew the serpent of matter and the serpent of illusion. If the serpent symbology is studied, we shall find that three serpents are depicted: one standing for the serpent of matter, another for the serpent of illusion, and the third for the serpent of wisdom. This last serpent is only discovered when the other two have been slain.

This sense of duality is the first stage of the spiritual experience and colours the thoughts of all the great aspirants and mystics of the world. Note how St. Paul cries out as he wrestles with the problem:

"I find then a law, that, when I would do good, evil is present with me.

"For I delight in the law of God after the inward man: But I see another law in my members, warring against the law of my mind, and bringing me into captivity to the law of sin which is in my members.

"I thank God through Jesus Christ our Lord. So then with the mind I myself serve the law of God; but with the flesh the law of sin". (*Romans; VII; 21-25*)

As Hercules grew up, we are told, great care was given to his education. He was trained in all possible accomplishments, and every faculty that he had was developed and organised. What is the lesson to be learned from this?   It is the need to realise that every disciple, if he truly merits that name, must necessarily be a highly developed member of the human family. All three parts of his nature have to be unfolded; his mind must be well-stocked and functioning, and he must know how to use it; his sensitive emotional nature must be responsive to every type of contact; his physical body must be a fit medium of expression for the indwelling soul and equipped to undertake the tasks to which the man has pledged himself.

There has been amongst aspirants for many centuries a tendency to decry and belittle the mind. They are apt to say glibly, "The mind is the slayer of the real", and, through an unrecognised mental inertia and laziness, to feel that the important thing is to have the heart nature developed. They regard the mind, with its capacity to analyse and discriminate, as a snare and a delusion. But this surely is an error. Knowledge of God is as necessary and as important as love of God; and this the new age, with its new type of aspirant, will most assuredly demonstrate. Saintliness, sweetness and a pleasing, loving disposition have their place in the sum-total of the characteristics

nt, but when linked to stupidity and an undeveloped
hey fail to be as useful as they could be when cou-
pleu ι. :lligence. When linked to a high grade intellect and
with mental powers oriented to divine knowledge, they will
produce that knower of God whose influence becomes world-
wide and who can both love and teach his fellowmen.

So Hercules was trained in all accomplishments and could
take his place with the thinkers of his time. We are told also that
his height was four cubits, a symbolic way of expressing the
fact that he had achieved his full growth in all departments of
his four-fold personality. Man, we are told, is the cube, "the city
that stands foursquare". Physically, emotionally and mentally,
he was developed and to these three factors is added a fourth,
a soul in conscious possession of its mechanism, the developed
personality.

Having achieved his growth and having been trained in all
that the world could give him, we are told next that he proceeded to slay his teachers. He killed them all and got rid of
them. Why? Because he had reached the point where he could
stand on his own feet, forming his own conclusions, guiding
his own life, and handling his own affairs. It was necessary,
therefore, to rid himself of all those who sought to supervise
him; he had to break away from authority and set out to find
his own way and make his own contacts with life. This is where
many aspirants stand at this time. They are in possession of
much theory, they have a relatively wide technical knowledge
of the nature of the Path and of what they should do upon it,
but they do not as yet stand on their own feet and tread that
Path, alone and unsupported. They need props, and look for
people to tell them what to do and what they should believe.
We shall find in the third labour which Hercules performed, in
the sign Gemini, that he was tested on this point and had to
prove that he was justified in taking this step. He then makes
the interesting discovery that he is not nearly so free nor so
strong as, in his youthful enthusiasm, he fancied himself to be.

When he reached the age of eighteen years, we are told, he slew a lion which was devastating the countryside and that he began to perform other public services, so that, little by little, his name came before the people. Eighteen is always a significant number. In it we have the number ten, which is the number of personality perfection, plus the number eight, which, we are told by some numerologists, is the number of the Christ force. It is the Christ force, in the new cycle of discipleship, seeking to express itself, which produces the condition of turmoil and the difficulties which characterise that stage. It is of value perhaps to note the following:

> "Number eight is the circle which we have already found to be the container of all the potencies out of which the Light shall bring Perfection, but now twisted or turned upon itself. The serpent no longer swallows its tail, thus completing its cycle, but writhes and twists in space and out of the contortions of its writhings it brings forth a perverted image of itself. . . But in eighteen we have the vision of the Straight and Narrow Path: the Dot has unfolded into the one and become the axis around which our life turns. At this step the Initiate has faced this one divine truth and felt the mighty urge of the One Life. Henceforth he strives to make the twisted line (8) subservient to the straight line (1)"(*The Key of Destiny*, H. A. and F. H. Curtiss, pp. 246-247).

It is interesting to note also that we are told in the Kabalah: "The eighteenth path is called the House of Influence ... and from the midst of the investigation the arcana and hidden sense are drawn forth which dwell in its shade and which cling to it from the cause of all causes". (*Sepher Yetzira*, No. 30).

This is what Hercules, at the age of eighteen, is setting out to do. He must tread the Path whereon all the hidden things can be brought forth into the light; he has reached the point where he can achieve knowledge of himself and can begin to investigate the hidden forces of nature. This is the problem of all disciples.

The next episode in his career is his marriage and the birth of three children, a symbolic way of expressing the truth that he made at-one-ment with Psyche, the soul. From that union the three aspects of the soul were born or began to manifest themselves. He began to know the nature of the spiritual will and to use it in the directing of his life. He experienced the workings of spiritual love and became conscious of the need to serve. Spiritual mind began to reveal truth to him and he saw the underlying purpose. These are the higher correspondences of the three aspects of the personality, his mind, his emotional nature, and his physical body.

We now discover him going through a very peculiar stage. We read in the ancient story that Hera (Psyche, or the soul) drove him mad. She drove him mad through jealousy and, whilst in that curious state, we read that he slew his children and his friends and everyone connected with him. May it not be suggested in this connection that he passed through that unwholesome state common to all beginners on the Path of Discipleship, in which a morbid conscientiousness sacrifices everybody and everything to individual soul unfoldment? This is a most common fault with aspirants. Their sense of proportion is frequently at fault and their sense of values distorted. The balanced and sane life, which is the ideal for a son of God, is subordinated to a fanatical determination to make spiritual progress. Spiritual ambition sways the aspirant and he becomes destructive, unbalanced and, usually, exceedingly difficult to live with. There is much sound counsel in the Biblical injunction, "Be not righteous overmuch, why shouldst thou die?" This stage is curiously exemplified for us on a large scale in the fanatical sacrifices made in the Orient, and under the Inquisition and the Protestant Covenanters, of all who interpreted truth contrary to the conviction of a particular group of believers.

Ecc 7:16

When Hercules had recovered from his insanity, as he fortunately did, we are told that a new name was given to him, that a new abode was assigned to him and that the twelve labours were laid upon him for fulfillment. We are told that these words were spoken to him: "From this day forth thy name shall no more be Alkeides, but Herakles. In Tirjus shalt thou make thy abode, and there, serving, thou shalt accomplish thy labours. When this shall be accomplished then thou shalt become one of the Immortals". (*Greek and Roman Mythology, Vol. I, Fox.*) Having recovered his sanity, the focus of his life was changed. He no longer lived down where he lived before. The name of the soul became his name, and he was constantly reminded thereby that to express the glory of the soul was his mission. The twelve great labours that were to set the seal of accomplishment upon his life, and which would indicate his right to join the great group of Immortals, were outlined to him and he entered upon the *Way*.

We are told that in his person he symbolised the Fixed Cross in the heavens, formed by the four constellations Taurus, Leo, Scorpio and Aquarius. Tradition tells us that he was physically bullnecked, as well as psychologically stubborn and ready to attack any problem and to rush blindly into any undertaking. Nothing could turn him from his purpose, and we shall see when we study the labours that he rushed headlong into them. Nothing deterred him, nothing frightened him, and one-pointedly he went his way. The ancient motto that has governed the activities of all active disciples became his and his soul enjoined upon him the need of "the power to do, the power to dare, the power to be silent, and the power to know". "The power to do" is the motto of Taurus, and this he exemplified in his twelve labours. He symbolised Leo, because he always wore the lion's skin as a proof of his courage, and the motto of that sign being "the power to dare", no danger affrighted him and no difficulty turned him back.

Perhaps his outstanding achievement was what he accomplished in the sign Scorpio; for the great work was to overcome illusion. It was consummated and carried to completion in the sign Scorpio. The motto of that sign is silence. In Capricorn he becomes the Initiate, and this stage is always impossible until illusion has been overcome and the power of silence has been achieved. Therefore, when an infant in the cradle, unable to speak, he symbolised the high water mark of his achievement by strangling the two serpents. Then, at his maturity, he symbolised in himself Aquarius the Man, whose motto is "to know". He had a mind and used his intellect in active work and service. So, doing and daring, in silence and with knowledge, he overcame all obstacles and passed undeterred from Aries to Pisces; starting in Aries as the humble aspirant and ending in Pisces as the all-knowing, victorious World Saviour.

One point might be made here. In the history of Hercules we are told nothing of what he ever said; we are only told of what he did. Through his deeds, he earned the right to speak. In the story of that greater Son of God, Jesus the Christ, we are told not only what he did but also what he said. In the silence of Hercules and in his steady accomplishment, no matter by what failure and difficulty he might be faced, and in his power of endurance, we have shown to us the characteristics of the disciple. In the story of Jesus the Christ, through the demonstration of his powers and by the words he spoke, we have the proofs of the Initiate.

And now having reached maturity, having evolved the characteristics necessary for his mission, we read that the gods and goddesses did their utmost to equip him for the work that he had to do. He had received all that the world could give him; now the powers of the soul were conferred upon him, and he had to learn how to use them. We read that Minerva gave him a beautiful robe but, as we never read of his wearing it, we can infer that something symbolic is intended. There are many cases in history where a robe is given: Joseph received a many-coloured garment from his father; the mantle of Elijah descended upon Elisha, and the robe of Christ was divided up and quarrelled over by the soldiers at the crucifixion. It is the general opinion that the robe is the symbol of vocation. The vocation of Elijah had passed on to Elisha; the vocation of the Christ, the World Saviour, came to an end at the crucifixion when he entered upon greater and more important work.

The wisdom that was now realised by Hercules because he had made the at-one-ment with the soul, impressed upon him a sense of vocation. He was pledged to the spiritual life and nothing could deter him. Vulcan gave him a golden breastplate, magnetic and protective, the symbol of energy, emanating from high sources of spiritual power, which will enable the aspirant to undertake the twelve labours and go forward unafraid. From Neptune, the god of the waters, he received horses. The symbology underlying this gift is very interesting. Horses, as well as Neptune, the god of the waters and the deity of the watery, emotional nature, stand for the capacity to be carried away by either a line of thought or an emotional reaction. This emotional, fluidic nature, with its sensitivity and its power to feel, when rightly used and subordinated to god-like purposes, is one of the greatest assets that the disciple possesses. With the aid of Neptune and the rapid steeds, Hercules could be *en rapport* with the most distant sphere in which his labours could be cast. Through emotional sensitivity and response, we, too, can be *en rapport* with the world in which our labours are cast. Equipped, therefore, with vocation, spiritual energy and sensitivity, the gift of a sword that came from Mercury, the messenger of the gods, is of profound significance, for the sword is the symbol of the mind which divides asunder, separates and cuts off. Through its use, Mercury added to the other gifts bestowed upon Hercules that of mental analysis and discrimination. We are told that Apollo, the Sun God himself, became interested in Hercules and pondered what he could give him that would serve him. Finally he gave him a bow and arrow, symbolising the capacity to go straight to the goal; symbol, too, of that piercing illumination, that shaft of Light which could irradiate the darkness of his path, when needed.

Thus equipped, Hercules stands ready for the great endeavour. And when all the gifts had been bestowed and he stood with his divine equipment, we read of a most intriguing little detail:

he went out and cut for himself a club. All these divine gifts were very lovely and wonderful but as yet he did not know how to use them. He sensed his vocation, he believed in spiritual energy, he was told that he possessed the horses of contact and that, if he would, the bow and arrow of illumination were his; but he liked the familiar club of his own fashioning. He would rather bludgeon his way through with what he knew he could use than use the unfamiliar tools which had been given him. So he clutched his wooden club and set out upon his labours.

LABOUR I. *Thought*

THE CAPTURE OF THE MAN-EATING MARES
(Aries, March 21st - April 20th)

The Myth

The first great Gate stood open wide. A voice came through that portal: "Hercules, my son, go forth. Pass through the Gate and enter on the *Way*. Perform thy labour and return to me, reporting on the deed".

HOPE

With shouts of triumph Hercules rushed forth, running between the pillars of the Gate with over-weening confidence and surety of power. And thus the Labour started and the first great act of service was begun. The story that they tell carries instruction for the sons of men, who are the sons of God.

The son of Mars, Diomedes of fiery fame, ruled in the land beyond the Gate, and there he raised the horses and the mares of war, upon the marshes of his land. Wild were these horses and fierce the mares and all men trembled at their sound, for they ravaged up and down the land, wreaking great damage, killing all the sons of men who crossed their path, and breeding steadily most wild and evil horses.

"Capture these mares, and stop these evil deeds", was the command which fell upon the ears of Hercules. "Go, rescue this far land and those who live upon it".

"Abderis", cried Hercules, "come forth and aid me with this task", calling the friend he greatly loved and who ever followed in his steps as he went from place to place. And Abderis came forth and took his stand beside his friend and with him faced the task. Laying all plans with care, these two followed the horses as they ranged the meadows and the marshes of that land. Finally, he cornered these wild mares within a field

wherein there was no further place to move, and there he caught
and tethered them. He yelled with joy at the success achieved.

So great was his delight in the prowess thus displayed that
he deemed it 'neath his dignity to hold the mares or drive them
on the *Way* to Diomedes. He called his friend, saying: "Abderis,
come hither and drive these horses through the Gate". And then
he turned his back and pridefully marched forward.

But Abderis was weak and feared the task. He could not
hold the mares, or harness them or drive them through the Gate
in the footsteps of his friend. They turned on him; they rent and
trod him underfoot; they killed him and escaped into the wilder
lands of Diomedes.

Wiser, grief-stricken, humble and discouraged, Hercules returned unto his task. He sought the mares again from place to
place, leaving his friend, dying upon the ground. Again he
caught the horses, and drove them through the Gate himself.
But Abderis lay dead.

The Teacher looked him o'er with care and sent the horses
to the place of peace, there to be tamed and broken to their
tasks. The people of that land, released from fear, welcomed
the deliverer; acclaiming Hercules as saviour of the land. But
Abderis lay dead.

The Teacher turned to Hercules and said: "Labour the first
is ended; the task is done, but badly done. Learn the true lesson
of this task and then pass on to further service to your fellowmen. Go forth into the country guarded by the second Gate and
find and take the sacred Bull into the Holy Place".

THE TIBETAN.

The Meaning of the Myth

In combining this astrological and symbolic story with the
everyday life and tests of modern discipleship, we shall tell the
story of the task which Hercules undertook, and the test to
which King Eurystheus subjected him; and then we shall study

the significance of the sign in which it took place, for there is a close link between the two, and the labour only became possible because of the characteristics conferred upon Hercules in that particular sign. Each sign subjects the man who is working in it to the influence of certain distinctive forces, and provides him with certain tendencies. These we must understand if the meaning of the test is to emerge.

Connected with each sign of the Zodiac will be found three other constellations, which symbolically (and often in a most amazing fashion) embody the disciple's problem and indicate the solution. These we shall have to consider; for the labour; the sign, and the allied constellations with the forces let loose through their combination, constitute a complete story which is full of instructive elements. I would like to point out for the sake of clarity, therefore, that the constellations symbolise the threefold spirit aspect; that the sign gives us the field of activity of the soul, and that the labour portrays the work of the disciple, living on the physical plane and endeavouring to demonstrate on the battlefield of the world his innate divinity and latent powers. In these three we have spirit, soul and body summarised. Life, consciousness and form meet in Hercules, the personal self, who, acting under the influence of the soul, the indwelling Christ, carries out the purposes of the Spirit, the Father in Heaven. We shall next consider the relationship of sign and constellations, and close each chapter with a definite application of the story of the test to the life of a disciple and to that of humanity as a whole.

In studying the twelve labours, we follow the career of Hercules as he passes around the Zodiac from the sign Aries, which is the sign of commencement, through Taurus, Gemini, etc. (anti-clockwise) to Pisces, the sign of death and of consummation. This will be in the reverse manner to that of the apparent path of the sun (clockwise) which is begun in Aries and appears then to retrograde through the signs, passing into Pisces, and then to Aquarius, and so on through all the intervening signs,

back again to Aries. The man who is immersed in form and is
living under the influence of the matter aspect follows necessarily the path of illusion and of appearances; but Hercules, the
soul, follows the true Way, reverses the usual procedure and,
figuratively speaking, goes against the tide. Hercules, the awakened soul, is realising the day of opportunity. He has received
his instructions to undertake the twelve labours and demonstrate
his capacities, and has been promised that if he fulfils the requirements he will be translated into the kingdom of the gods.
He has been equipped with all divine powers, though, as yet,
he does not know how to use them, and he has hewn out for
himself the club of his own endeavour; and with these he symbolically mounts the cross: the fixed cross of the heavens, upon
which he remains in spirit until the last labour has been accomplished.

Thus he sets out on his first labour, little realising the magnitude of his task, and unprepared for failure. The delightful
part of the story of Hercules is his impulsiveness and the fact
that he was not always successful. He failed sometimes and had
to re-do the labour until success followed on his efforts.

He is told that Diomedes, the son of Mars, the god of war,
possesses a large number of brood mares. These were running
wild, devastating the countryside, doing much damage and
subsisting on the flesh of human beings. No one was safe from
them and terror had settled down on the neighbourhood. Besides this, these brood mares were breeding great numbers of
war horses, and Diomedes was very concerned with the out-
come of the situation. Eurystheus, the King, ordered Hercules
to capture them. Many attempts had been made to do so, but
always the mares had escaped after killing the horses and men
sent against them. But Hercules, having caught the horses,
gave them to Abderis to hold, whilst he strutted on ahead, not
realising the strength of the horses, nor their savagery. Before
he could take steps to prevent it, the mares turned on Abderis
and trampled him to death, and again escaped and started anew

to ravage the countryside. So he had to start his labour all over again, and after strenuous efforts he again succeeded in capturing the mares. This first labour, therefore, starts with a partial failure, as is so often the case with the inexperienced and impetuous aspirant. Such is the story, brief, dramatic and encouraging. What of the sign in which it was undertaken?

The Sign

The sign Aries, which was the field of this first activity, is always spoken of as the first sign of the Zodiac. At this sign the great wheel begins its cyclic turning. It is, therefore, the sign of commencement. Cosmically speaking, it is the sign of creation, and this thought underlies the words in the Bible, "The Lamb slain from the foundation of the world," (*Rev. XIII,* 8) for this sign is called the sign of the Ram or of the Lamb. In the life of the human being it marks the beginning of the first subjective, latent consciousness of existence, and the start of the human being upon the circle of experience. In the life of the aspirant to discipleship it connotes the period of re-orientation and of a renewed self-conscious effort, and his start upon that final stage of the evolutionary path which will carry him out of the human kingdom and enable him to make the transition into the kingdom of the gods. Such is the promise made to Hercules and such is the reward held out to all disciples. This first labour marks the first step upon the "path of translation".

Aries is the sign of out-going power; of the streaming forth of divine energy from the central deity, God, or from the human being, a son of God. This energy streams forth in two directions (thus the point becomes the line, the One becomes the first): it streams forth into the world of forms, and also into the world of being or of spirit. One stream of energy expresses the path of return, of inward-going, and the two together constitute the two arcs of the great circle of existence. In this sign starts the path on which form is taken and dominates; on it likewise begins the life of inner unfoldment and the domination of the soul, or of subjective Being. Re-organisation, reorientation, re-polarising and regeneration, are the characteristics of this stage, and all of them are expressions of the same life force. The two uses of this force are dependent upon the mental attention of the being, divine and human, who is utilising it. It is the same force, but used in two different ways, dependent upon whether the divine user has focused his attention upon form-taking, or upon treading the path of liberation from form.

For aeons, this life force has been applied to selfish ends, to the purposes of self-gratification and to the satisfaction of desire. Little by little form-life loses its attraction until, having passed around and around the zodiacal wheel, the man finds himself back again in Aries, only this time with a new focus, a fresh interest and a different vision. He has had held before him the promise that, having achieved certain objectives, he may cease from incarnating and attain the kingdom of the gods; he has learned from experience something of his own essential duality and yearns to cease from satisfying the lower aspect of that duality and to meet the need of the higher; and he is beginning to respond to impulses coming from the world of souls, and to vision group ends and group objectives. Now he has to learn to use the life force with unselfish intent, and not for the satisfaction of his personal greeds.

The Three Initial Impulses in Aries

Three outstanding urges characterise this sign. There is, as we have seen, the urge to begin. This may express itself simply as the urge to take form, to become involved in matter; or it may reverse the process and focus itself in the urge to achieve liberation from form, and the emergence of the soul from the prison of the form nature. Then this urge is followed by the consequent urge to create, that activity of the Deity which results in the formation of worlds of expression and satisfies His desire to incarnate in a solar system, and to begin the great life cycle

Aries energy → Impulse

of the universe. It may be likewise the urge to individual creation, of the soul to take a body, or of a human being to create something which shall be specially his own. In ancient Accadian days, this sign Aries was called that "wherein the sacrifice of righteousness was made", or the sign of "the fallen angels". The sons of God, impelled by this basic urge, fell from their high estate, took form, and started upon their individual round upon round of the Zodiac.

Thirdly, we find the urge to resurrection. In Aries, which has seen the beginning of form life and which has initiated the creative work, there begins to be felt the urge to achieve freedom from the form, to roll away the stone from the door of the sepulchre of the soul, and to stand in the liberty of the sons of God. In Aries is found the impulse which leads to the building of the form, which for ages will constitute the prison house of the soul. This reaches its mass form in Cancer; and its human form in Leo; the densest point of illusion in form is reached in Scorpio, and in Pisces the form dies, only to be rebuilt again in the wearying round of form experience. But in this sign the Way of Liberation is first sensed, and the building of the spiritual body is begun. This is the sign of germinal spiritual activity, which later leads to the birth of the Christ child, in Virgo, to that of the world Saviour; in Capricorn and in Pisces. Physical commencement and spiritual commencement, physical creation and spiritual creation, physical emergence and spiritual liberation: these are the initial impulses sensed in Aries.

It is the sign, therefore, of strong and potent impulses, and of violent fluctuations and exaggerated efforts; often a sign of failure, but always of ultimate success. In its opposite sign Libra, it reaches its consummation of balance and of equilibrium, for the intervening experience and the lessons learned from the intermediate five labours bring about that poise and balanced attitude which we shall note in Hercules when he captures the Boar, in Libra...

In the Brahmanical zodiac, Vishnu presides over Aries and Vishnu is the second person of the Hindu Trimurti, or the cosmic Christ in incarnation, as he initiates the process of form-taking, and ultimately brings about the final episode of resurrection. Thus Vishnu or Christ embodies the two urges, the urge to create and build form and the urge to liberation, or resurrection out of form. It is under this urge to liberation that Hercules starts upon his labours.

The Sign of the Mind

Aries governs the head. It is consequently the sign of the thinker and, therefore, a powerful mental sign. All beginnings originate on the mental plane and in the mind of the creator, whether that creator is God or the soul of man. This universe had its origin in the thought of God, the cosmic Thinker. The soul started its career in matter through the same process of thought. The human family, the fourth kingdom in nature, came into being when mind emerged and differentiated man from the animals. The aspirant begins his labours when he truly becomes the thinker; and in full awareness proceeds to function as the arbiter of his own destiny. ...

It is apparent, consequently, that in Aries right direction and right orientation have their beginning, and Hercules, the newly-thinking disciple, begins his work. The key to this labour and to the significance of the sign is to be found in the words of an ancient Indian scripture: "Man does not rightly know the way to the heavenly world, but the horse does rightly know it". In the very ancient days in India, the horse sacrifice was linked with the sun god, and, yearly, we are told, the sun god, as the zodiacal horse, was supposed by the Vedic Aryans to die to save all flesh. The sun chariot of Apollo is depicted as drawn by horses, and the "princely sign of the Ram" is closely connected with the horse symbology, a fact to which this first labour bears witness.

Reference to books on symbology will show us that the horse

stands for intellectual activity. The white horse symbolises the illumined mind of the spiritual man, and so we find in the Book of Revelations that Christ comes forth riding upon a white horse. Black horses represent the lower mind, with its false ideas and erring human concepts. The brood mares, such as we meet in this first labour, indicate the feminine aspect of the mind as it gives birth to ideas, to theories and to concepts. The thought-form making tendency of the mind is here symbolised, embodying the ideas conceived, and which are let loose upon the world, devastating and destroying when emanating from the lower mind, but constructing and saving when coming from the soul.

The exoteric ruler of this sign is Mars, the god of war, and so Hercules, acting under the right direction of thought and beginning his work on the mental plane, takes his stand as the warrior. His outstanding characteristic in this sign is the pioneering, militant spirit. The mares were in the possession of Diomedes, the son of Mars. (But the esoteric ruler is Mercury, which "illumines the mind and mediates between the soul and the personality.")

Constellations in Aries

As is usual, there are three constellations connected with Aries. First, there is Cassiopeia, the Enthroned Queen, the symbol always of matter. It is most interesting to note how in the circle of the Zodiac we come across three women. In connection with Aries, the sign of commencement, we find Cassiopeia, the Dominant Woman. Woman and Child and as we shall later see, mother-matter is the nurturer of the infant Christ, the Virgin Mary gives birth to Jesus. In Pisces, at the close of the great round, we find Andromeda, the Chained Woman. First the woman enthroned and dominant, then the woman caring for the infant, Christ, and then the woman, representing matter that has been dominated and controlled. Cassiopeia will be found seated on the Arctic Circle, close to

Cepheus the King, or Lawgiver, whom we shall meet later as one of the three constellations in Pisces. At the commencement, Law; at the close, Law; for Cepheus has a close relation with the first and the last sign of the Zodiac. It is interesting to note that Mahomet, the founder of the most militant religion, was born in this sign, and legend says that Moses also was born in it; Moses, the lawgiver, and Mahomet, the warrior.

The problem of Hercules, as he enters upon his labours, is to demonstrate his power over matter and form, and so he has to recognise Cassiopeia from the very beginning, the hitherto enthroned queen.

The second constellation is Cetus, the Sea Monster, the Enemy of Little Fishes... One of the great symbols of the soul is the fish swimming in the ocean of matter, and Cetus, the sea monster, is the symbol of what we call evil, that seeks to destroy the soul in incarnation. The sea monster, in the ocean of existence, and the enthroned queen, spoke to Hercules of the magnitude of his problem, but the third constellation spoke to him of victory. Perseus is the third of the three constellations, called in the zodiac of Denderah, in Egypt, "the one who subdues"; sometimes called "the breaker", that which can chain the enthroned woman, and that which can conquer the monster. We are told that Perseus possessed the helmet of invisibility, the sandals of swiftness, the buckler of wisdom and the sword of the spirit. Thus Hercules saw himself reflected in the heavens, and as he started upon the capture of the man-eating mares, he discovered in himself the guarantee of his ultimate achievement, even though at the time the difficulties with which he was faced seemed insuperable.

The Crux of the Test   *Larger Goal*

The conquest of matter and the overcoming of illusion loomed large before Hercules and indicated from the very outset of the twelve labours the nature of his final achievement. It has been said that the keynote of the sign Aries is hope and, as he faced his twelve labours, hope was all the guarantee that Hercules then had that he would achieve. Hope, his untried divine equipment, his personal club, and much enthusiasm: so start all disciples.

The meaning of the test is now surely plain. Hercules had to begin in the world of thought to gain mental control. For ages the brood mares of thought had been breeding war horses and, through wrong thought, wrong speech and erroneous ideas, had been devastating the countryside. One of the first lessons that every beginner has to learn is the tremendous power that he mentally wields, and the amount of harm that he can cause in his neighbourhood and environment through the brood mares of his mind. He has, therefore, to learn the right use of his mind, and the first thing that he has to do is capture this feminine aspect of the mind and see to it that no more war horses are bred. Any would-be Hercules can easily prove that he possesses these devastating brood mares, if for one entire day he pays close attention to his thoughts and to the words he speaks, which are ever the result of thought. He will rapidly discover that selfishness, unkindness, love of gossip, and criticism constitute a large part of his thought content and that the brood mares of his mind are constantly being fertilised by selfishness and illusion. Instead of these brood mares giving birth to ideas and concepts which have their origin in the kingdom of the soul, and instead of being fertilised from the spiritual realm, they become the parents of error, falseness and cruelty, which have their origin in the lower aspects of man's nature.

Hercules realised the harm that the brood mares were doing. He rushed gallantly to the rescue of his neighbourhood. He determined to capture the brood mares, but he overestimated himself. He did succeed in rounding them up and in capturing them, but he failed to realise their potency and strength, so he gave them to Abderis, the symbol of the lower personal self, to hold. But Hercules, the soul, and Abderis, the personality, in

the personality CANNOT handle the construction of the soul

unison were needed to guard these devastating horses. Abderis alone was not strong enough, and what had been happening to the people in the neighbourhood, happened to Abderis; they killed him. This is an instance of the working of the great law that we pay the price in our own natures of wrongly-spoken words and ill-judged actions. Again the soul, in the person of Hercules, had to deal with the problem of wrong thought, and only, when he becomes a one-pointed aspirant in the sign Sagittarius and in that sign kills the Man-Eating Birds, does he really attain complete control of the thought processes of his nature.

The practical significance of the power of thought has been well expressed for us in the words of Thackeray: "Sow a thought, and reap an action. Sow an action, and reap a habit. Sow a habit, and reap character. Sow character and reap destiny".

(The two key-words of the sign Aries are:*

    1. "And the Word said: Let form again be sought".

The Man.

    2. "I come forth and from the plane of mind, I rule".

The Initiate.)

(*From *Esoteric Astrology,* Volume III of *A Treatise on the Seven Rays*, p. 108. Received three years after A.A.B. gave the Hercules lectures in New York.)

LABOUR II. *Desire*

THE CAPTURE OF THE CRETAN BULL
(Taurus, April 21st-May 20th)

The Myth

The presiding One spoke to the Teacher of the man whose light shone forth among the sons of men, who are the sons of God.

"Where is the man who stood with power before the Gods, received their gifts and entered through the first wide open Gate to labour at his task."

"He rests, Oh, great presiding One, and ponders on his failure, and mourns for Abderis, and seeks for help within himself".

"It is well. The gifts of failure guarantee success, when rightly understood. Let him proceed to labour once again, enter the second Gate, returning with dispatch".

The second Gate stood open wide and, from the light which veiled the distant scene, a voice emerged and said: "Pass through the Gate. Proceed upon thy way. Perform thy labour and return to me, reporting on the deed".

Alone and sad, conscious of need and worn with deep distress, Hercules slowly passed between the pillars of the Gate into the light which shines where stands the sacred bull. On the horizon rose the island fair where dwelt the bull, and where adventurous men could enter that vast maze which lured them to bewilderment, the maze of Minos, King of Crete, the keeper of the bull.

Crossing the ocean to the sunlit isle (though how we are not told) Hercules entered on his task to seek and find the bull, and lead it to the Holy Place where dwell the one-eyed men. From place to place he chased the bull, led by the gleaming star which shone upon the forehead of the bull, a bright lamp in a dark place. This light, moving as moved the bull, led him from place to place. Alone, he sought the bull; alone he chased it to its lair; alone he captured it and mounted on its back. Around him stood the Sisters seven, urging him on his way and, in the shining light, he rode the bull across the glimmering water to the isle of Crete unto the land where dwelt the Cyclops three.

These three great sons of God awaited his return, watching his progress through the waves. He rode the bull as if it were a horse, and with the Sisters singing as he went, drew near unto the land.

"He comes with strength", said Brontes, and went to meet him on the shore.

"He rides in light", said Steropes, "his inner light will brighter be", then fanned the light to sudden flame.

"He comes with speed", said Arges, "he is riding through the waves."

Hercules nearer drew, urging the sacred bull upon the *Way*, throwing the light upon the trail which led from Crete unto the Temple of the Lord, within the city of the one-eyed men. Upon the mainland, at the water's edge, these three men stood and grasped the bull, taking it thus away from Hercules.

"What hast thou here?" said Brontes, arresting Hercules upon the *Way*.

"The sacred bull, Oh, Holy One".

"Who art thou? Tell us now thy name", said Steropes.

"I am the son of Hera, a son of man and yet a son of God. I have performed my task. Take now the bull into the Holy Place and save it from due death. Minos desired its sacrifice".

"Who told you thus to seek and save the bull?" said Arges, moving towards the Holy Place."

"Within myself I felt the urge and sought my Teacher. Told by the great Presiding One, He sent me on the *Way* and with long search and many pains, I found the bull. Helped by its holy light, I rode it through the separating sea unto this Holy Place.

"Depart in peace, my son, your task is done".

The Teacher saw him coming and went forth to meet him on the *Way*. Across the waters came the voices of the Sisters seven, singing around the bull, and nearer still the chanting of the one-eyed men within the Temple of the Lord, high in the Holy Place.

"You came with empty hands, oh, Hercules", the Teacher said.

"I have these empty hands, because I have fulfilled the task to which I was assigned. The sacred bull is rescued, securely with the Three. What next?"

"Within the light shall you see light; walk in that light and there see light. Your light must brighter shine. The bull is in the Holy Place".

And Hercules reposed upon the grass and rested from his labour. Later the Teacher turned to Hercules and said: "Labour the second is performed, and easy was the task. Learn from this task the lesson of proportion. Strength to perform the arduous task; a willingness to do the task which taxes not your powers; such are two lessons learnt. Rise soon and seek the country, guarded by Gate the third, and find the golden apples. Bring them here".

THE TIBETAN.

The Meaning of the Labour

In spite of an initial partial failure, Hercules has made his start. In line with the universal law he has begun his work on the mental plane.

In the working out of the creative plan, thought-impulse is followed by desire. That state of consciousness, which we call mental, is succeeded by the state of sensitivity, and this second labour deals with the desire world and with the potency of desire. It is one of the most interesting labours and one that is told us in fullest detail. Some of the accounts given of the various tests to which Hercules was subjected are exceedingly sketchy and brief in outline, but the tests in Taurus and Gemini, in Scorpio and Pisces, are related at greater length. They were drastic in their application and tried out every part of the aspirant's nature.

The key to the labour in Taurus is the right understanding of the law of Attraction. This is the law that governs that magnetic force and that principle of coherence which builds the forms through which God, or the soul, manifests. It produces the stability which demonstrates in the persistence of the form throughout its cycle of existence, and concerns the interrelation between that which builds the form and the form itself; between the two poles, positive and negative; between spirit and matter; between the Self and the not-Self; between male and female, and thus between the opposites. *FORM*

Four Symbolic Words

We find that this test concerns predominantly the problem of sex. There are four words in the English language which are ideographic and symbolic. They consist of three letters each and are as follows: God, Sex, Law and Sin. In these four words we find expressed the sum total of all that is.

God, the sum total of all forms, the sum total of all states of consciousness, and the energising Life. *Sex,* that Life in operation, attracting spirit and matter and instituting the interplay between the objective and the subjective and between the exoteric and the esoteric. *Sex,* desire, attraction, the instinctive urge to creation, the pull of the soul, the urge to divinity, desire of the male for the female, the lure of matter for spirit; all these phrases can be piled up to express some of the activities of Sex in its various relations. *Law,* the thought-impelled response of God to form; the habits instituted by the timeless interplay between the polar opposites which have been recognised by humanity as the inevitable laws of nature; the imposition of the will of God and the impress of that will upon form and its recognition by man. *Sin,* according to its connotation, signifies "the one who it is", the uprising of the unit against the whole, individuality versus the group, selfishness instead of universal interest.

Thus is the story of the universe written for us in these four words. God, the Whole; Sex, the attraction between the parts within that Whole; Law, the habit of the Whole; and Sin, the revolt of the unit in the Whole.

The Story of the Labour

Minos, King of Crete, possessed a sacred bull, which he kept on the island of Crete. Eurystheus sent for Hercules and told him that it was necessary to capture the bull and bring it from the island to the mainland. No instructions were given as to how this was to be accomplished, and all that Hercules knew was that the bull was sacred, that it was born from the sea, and that its destiny was to be offered in sacrifice to Minos. Hercules, therefore, travelled to Crete and searched all over the island, pursuing the bull from place to place until at last he cornered it. Then, we are told, he rode the bull, like a horse, across the island and through the waters which separated Crete from the mainland, and so brought it into the city of the Cyclops. These Cyclops were peculiar beings of whom it was claimed that they possessed only one eye, set in the middle of the forehead. They were ruled over by three outstanding figures, whose names were Brontes, meaning thunder, Steropes, meaning lightning, and Arges, meaning whirling activity. When Hercules arrived with the bull at the gates of the city, he was met by the three Cyclops, who received the sacred bull from him and took charge of it. And thus ended the second labour.

The Theme of Illumination

Taurus is one of the most interesting of the zodiacal constellations, especially at this time. It is the Fixed Cross in the heavens, the Cross of the Disciple, and the following extract is of interest in this connection:

"The 'sky is mystically spoken of as the Temple, and the eternal consciousness of God. Its altar is the sun, whose four arms or rays typify the four corners of the cardinal cross of the universe,' which have become the four fixed signs of the zodiac, and as the four powerful sacred animal signs are both cosmical and spiritual, they represent the basic elements resembling our human principles. The sign Leo represents fire or spirit; Taurus, earth or body; Aquarius, air or mind; and Scorpio represents water likened to the soul. Leo, as the lion, is the strength of the lower nature, and is the serpent of force which, if directed upward, overcomes. Taurus, the bull, is always the symbol of creative force. Aquarius, the man, is the light-bearer, or light-bringer. Scorpio, the scorpion, is often transmuted with Aquila, the eagle... which rises at the same time with Scorpio; they are closely linked in symbolism. Scorpio is 'the monster of darkness,' who stings to death, and yet preserves and reproduces, symbolising not only generation but regeneration. As the latter it is Aquila, the eagle, the bird of the sun which has conquered the dark side of Scorpio (that adversary that can drag man down lower than the beasts), but when transmuted is the eagle of light, which can exalt above the gods".

The Celestial Ship of the North, Vol. I. (E. V. Straiton).

The "eye of the bull" in Taurus, the magnificent fixed star, Aldebaran, is one of the reasons why this constellation is regarded as conferring illumination. In ancient days it was called the leading star of the heavens, and Taurus has always been connected with light and, therefore, with Christ, who proclaimed himself as the Light of the World. Light, illumination and sound, as an expression of the creative force: these are the three basic ideas connected with this constellation. The "interpreter of the divine voice", as Taurus was called in ancient Egypt, can be paraphrased into Christian terminology and called "the Word made flesh". It is an interesting sidelight on the power of the zodiacal influences to recall that the bull's-eye lantern can be traced back to the bull's eye in Taurus, and the pontifical bull, or the papal enunciations which were regarded as interpreters of God's voice, is a term in common usage today.

It might well be asked here, in what way does Taurus, the bull, become the bringer of illumination? We are told that in this sign the moon is exalted and Venus is the ruler. The moon has always, from the standpoint of the esotericist, and among primitive agricultural peoples, been regarded as the form-building aspect. The moon is the symbol, therefore, of matter and is seen in many of our churches, closely connected with the Virgin Mary.

The consummation of the work that is undertaken in Taurus, and the result of the Taurian influence, is the glorification of matter and subsequent illumination through its medium. All that at present prevents the glory, which is the soul, and the radiance which emanates from the God within the form, from shining forth in its full power, is the matter or form aspect. When that has been consecrated, purified and spiritualised, then the glory and the light can indeed shine through and the moon aspect can, therefore, be exalted in Taurus. This is done through the influence of Venus, the symbol of earthly and of heavenly love, of both spiritual aspiration and of carnal desire, and is fittingly, therefore, the ruler of this sign. She is, above everything else, love, the creator of beauty and rhythm and unity. The bull and the cow together represent creation, and so Taurus and Venus are closely linked. The following is of interest:

"The bull or cow is the symbol of this sign, and in the celestial chart it will be observed that the little group of stars called Pleiades are represented just at the shoulder of the bull. Now, in Egyptian sculpture, or painting, the Pleiades are sometimes represented by the figure of a dove with wings outspread over the bull's saddle. The dove as we remember, is the bird sacred to Venus, and as the Pleiades are part of the constellation Taurus and, as we shall see, more Taurean in nature, if possible, than Taurus itself, the dove becomes a specially appropriate symbol for this little star-group".

The Zodiac: A Life Epitome, p. 24 (Walter H. Sampson)

The Theme of Sex

From this extract and many others which could be adduced, it is apparent how closely linked with sex, in its lower and in its higher aspects, is this important constellation of Taurus. This is why it has been called in some books, the "sign of generation", both earthly and heavenly. We have seen that the power of the sign Taurus is that of attraction, or of bringing together. It exerts a steady and continuous pull and in both the symbolical and the astronomical sense it attracts. We have seen that in this sign are to be found the Pleiades, among them Alcyone, called the central sun of our universe, and around it circles our sun, with its attendant planets. The words of Job when he said: "Canst thou bind the sweet influences of Pleiades or loose the bands of Orion?" thus become clear. The Pleiades are the symbol of the soul around which the wheel of life revolves.

It is interesting to discover again, in Taurus, the triplicity which is so constantly recurrent in astronomical lore and in mythology: Taurus, representing form and the attractive pull of matter; the Pleiades, representing soul and the vast recurring cycle of experience; and, among the seven Pleiades,* the Lost Pleiad (for only six are visible) a symbol of the obscuration of spirit, whilst soul, through desire, takes a body. Thus the idea of the relation of the Self and the not-Self, in order to produce the ultimate revelation of the spirit, underlies all mythological teaching and the scriptures and symbols of all time, and thus we have also the emergence of the idea of the great illusion and glamour. Spirit or God is "lost", or veiled, and disappears in the attractiveness of the outer form and in the glamour which the soul attracts around itself.

It should be remembered here that the opposite sign to Taurus is that of Scorpio, and these two signs constitute the

---

*Note the "seven Sisters" singing about Hercules, in the statement of the Myth.

field of a stupendous effort on the part of Hercules; for in one he wrestles with the problem of sex, and in the other, he overcomes the great illusion.

Significance of the Constellations

The three constellations connected with this sign are Orion, Eridanus, Auriga; and the nature of the work in Taurus is beautifully foretold by the three pictures in the heavens which they present to us. The ancient name of Orion was "the Three Kings", because of the three beautiful stars found in Orion's Belt. The Three Kings represent the three divine aspects of Will, Love and Intelligence, and Orion, therefore, symbolises the spirit. The name Orion literally means "the breaking forth of light".

Again and again, as we circle around the zodiac, shall we find appearing what might be called "the spiritual prototype" of Hercules; Perseus, the Coming Prince, who slew the Medusa, symbol of the great illusion. He is found in Aries; Orion, whose name means "light", is found in Taurus; in Scorpio, Hercules himself, triumphant and victorious, appears. Then we have Sagittarius, the Archer on the Horse, going straight for his goal, and in Pisces we find the King. The more closely we study this heavenly picture book, the more we realise that ever before us is held the symbol of our divinity, the symbol of the soul in incarnation, and the story of matter, as it receives purification and glorification through the laborious work of the soul.

The second constellation connected with this sign is an immense river of stars, which streams forth from under the feet of Orion. It is called Eridanus, or the "River of the Judge", and is a symbol of the river of life, carrying souls into incarnation, where they learn the meaning of the words, "as a man sows, so shall he reap", and where they undertake the stupendous task of working out their own salvation. Just as Orion

symbolises the spirit aspect, so Eridanus concerns itself with
the form-taking aspect and holds before us the thought of incarnation; whilst the third constellation, Auriga, is the chario-
teer, leading forth to new lands and so symbolising the soul.

Nature of the Tests

The broad lesson to be learned in this sign is to achieve
right understanding of the law of attraction and right use and
control of matter. In this way matter is raised up into heaven,
figuratively speaking, and can enter upon its right function;
which is, to constitute a medium of expression and a field of
endeavour for the indwelling Christ or soul. The aspirant, therefore, is tested in two ways: first as to the calibre of his animal
nature and the motives underlying its utilisation; second, he is
tested as to the attraction which the great illusion can exert over
him. Maya, or the great illusion, and sex are but two aspects of
the same force, that of attraction: one, as it manifests on the
physical plane, and the other, as it expresses itself in the field
of the emotional-desire nature.

The Disciple and Sex

An aspirant to discipleship has in sex a real problem with
which to contend. Self-indulgence and the control of the human
being by any part of his organism are always inevitably wrong.
When a man's entire mind is occupied with the thought of
women, or vice versa; when he lives mainly to satisfy an animal
craving; when he finds himself unable to resist the lure of his
polar opposite, then he is a victim of and is controlled by the
lowest part of his nature, the animal.

But when man recognises his physical functions as a divine
heritage, and his equipment as having been given him for the
good of the group and to be rightly used for the benefit of the
human family, then we shall see a new motivating impulse underlying human conduct where sex is concerned. We shall see
the elimination of promiscuity, with its attendant evil, disease.

We shall see the solution of the problem of too many children and, incidentally, easement of the economic problem. Through right control of the sex function and its relegation to the purpose for which it exists (the carrying onward of the human family and the providing of bodies whereby souls can gain experience) then right use will be made of sex. Then, passion, lust, self-gratification, disease, and overpopulation will die out in the world. Matter will no longer be prostituted to selfish desire, and the relation between the sexes will be governed by understanding of divine purpose and skill-in-action.

Two points of view are equally wrong: in the one case we have practices taught which lead eventually to sexual orgies. These have been dignified by the name of sex magic, and in the sexual orgasm, deliberately induced, a man is led to believe that the physical sex act is his highest point of spiritual opportunity and that, at such a moment, he can touch, if he will, the kingdom of Heaven.

The other attitude, which makes marriage and all expression of the sex life a sin for a disciple and which says that a man cannot be pure in the truly spiritual aspect if he marries and raises a family, is as devastatingly dangerous. There is no state of consciousness and no condition of life in which it is impossible for a man to function as a son of God. If it is not possible for a man to live the life of discipleship and the life of initiation and, with due self-control and understanding, live a normal, balanced sex life; then there *is* a department of human expression in which divinity is helpless, and this I refuse to recognise. There is no department of life, no field of expression, no meeting of obligation, no use of the physical apparatus, in which the soul cannot fulfill the part of the dominating factor and all things be done truly to the glory of God. But the soul must control, and not the lower nature. People forget that some of the greatest of the world initiates married; that the Buddha married and had a son, and must have been an initiate of high degree when he entered into the married state.

ιney forget that Moses, David the Psalmist, and many of the outstanding figures in the world of mysticism in both hemispheres, were married and raised families.

Disciples belong to all races, both in the occident and in the orient, and the attitude of different races towards sex is widely diversified. Standards of conduct differ. The legality or the illegality of relations varies. Different epochs and different civilisations have seen relationships that were legal at one time, and illegal at another. Some races are monogamous and some races are polygamous. In some civilisations the woman is regarded as the dominant factor, and in others the man. Down the ages sex perverts, homosexuals, true and spurious, have been with us, and today is probably no worse than 5,000 years ago, except that everything is now dragged out into the light, which is good. Everybody talks about the problem; and the rising generation are asking in no uncertain tones: "What about sex? What is right and what is wrong?" How can they be expected to deal with a question which has been discussed, seemingly in the most futile manner, down the ages?

Here it is pertinent to note that Minos, King of Crete, who owned the sacred bull also possessed the maze in which the Minotaur lived, and the maze has ever been the symbol of the great illusion. The word "maze" comes from an old English word, meaning to bewilder, to confuse, to puzzle. The island of Crete with its maze and its bull is an outstanding symbol of the great illusion. It was separated from the mainland, and illusion and bewilderment are characteristics of the separated self, but not of the soul on its own plane, where group realities and universal truths constitute its kingdom. The bull, to Hercules, typified animal desire, and the many aspects of desire in the world of form which, in their totality, constitute the great illusion. The disciple, like Hercules, is a separated unit, divided from the mainland, the symbol of the group, by the world of illusion and the maze in which he lives. The bull of desire has to be caught and mastered and chased from one point to another in the life of the separated self, until the time comes when the aspirant can do what Hercules succeeded in doing: ride the bull. To ride an animal, in the ancient myths, signifies control. *The bull is not slaughtered, it is ridden and guided, and under the mastery of the man.*

There are potencies and faculties hidden in the human being that, when developed and unfolded, may bring new powers to bear upon this problem. But, in the meantime, what shall the aspirant do? Certain suggestions may be made:

1. *Ride, control and master the bull,* and let the aspirant remember that the bull has to be ridden across the waters to the mainland; which means that the solution of the whole sex problem will come when the disciple subordinates his separated personal island self to group purpose and endeavour, and begins to rule his life by the question, "What is best for the group with which I am associated?" It is by doing this that the bull is ridden to the mainland.

2. *Use commonsense.* The ancient meaning of the word "commonsense" was that there was a sense which synthesised and unified the five senses and so constituted a "common sense", literally, the mind. Let the aspirant use his mind, and through the medium of intelligent perception, guide and control the bull of desire. If commonsense is used, certain dangers will be avoided. There is a danger in the method of many aspirants in inhibiting or shutting off all sex expression. Physiologically they may succeed, but the experience of psychologists and teachers is that where inhibition and a drastic suppression is imposed upon the organism, the result is some form of nervous or mental complex. Many physically clean people have unclean minds. Many who would scorn the practise of any of the sex perversions and who hold that marriage is not for the disciple, have mental apparatuses which will not bear investigation. Their minds and their interpretations of other people's actions are so salacious and their capacity to think evil so great, that, dangerous as this may sound, one feels that it would be better

for them to be ridden by the bull of desire than to continue their present practice of substituting mental indulgence for outer sin. A clean mind and a pure heart, a rightly organised and rightly used physical body, conformity to the laws of the land in which his destiny is cast, utter consideration for the welfare of those with whom he is associated, and a life of loving service: these constitute the ideals of the aspirant.

3. *A right understanding of the meaning of celibacy.* The word means "single", and the meaning usually given to the word is, to refrain from the marriage relation. Many young men and women, driven by spiritual desire and under the influence of the thoughtform of the church during the Middle Ages, with its many monasteries and convents, believe that for them the celibate state is essential and right, and are puzzled when they find that complexes result. But may it not be that the true celibacy has been expressed for us in the words of Christ, when he said, "If thine eye be single, thy whole body shall be full of light?" May it not be that true celibacy is the refusal of the soul any longer to identify itself with the form? May not the real marriage relation, of which the physical plane relation is but the symbol, be that of the union of the soul and the form, the positive spirit aspect and the negative mother-matter?

Let the soul be single in its purpose and freed from the thraldom of matter, and then right action and a right point of view will inevitably be the characteristics of the physical plane life. Let the soul ride the form, controlling and mastering it, and then it will surely know its right obligations. It will recognise the relation that it should hold to other human beings, whether its destiny is to be that of husband or wife, father or mother, brother or sister, friend or companion. Through right use of the form and right understanding of purpose, through right orientation to reality and right use of spiritual energy, the soul will act as the controlling factor and the whole body will be full of light. Through control, through the use of commonsense, by a right understanding of celibacy, and by identification with group purpose, the disciple will arrive at liberation from the control of sex. He will succeed in following the example of Hercules and will ride the bull of desire over to the mainland where, in the Temple of God, he will hand it over into the care of the Cyclops who were early initiates, having the single eye about which we have been speaking, the eye of Shiva, the Bull's eye in the constellation Taurus. For Hercules himself was not only the disciple, but he was, in his lower nature, the bull, and in his higher nature the Cyclops.

When the bull of desire has been handed over to the Cyclops, to the initiate with the single eye, which is himself, the soul, the three divine aspects, will begin to manifest: Brontes, Steropes and Arges will guard the sacred bull, and Hercules, the disciple, will no longer have any responsibility. Brontes is the symbol of the first aspect of God, the Father who spoke and is the creative sound. Steropes means lightning, or light, and is the second aspect, the soul. Arges means whirling activity, the third aspect of divinity, expressing itself in the intense activity of physical plane life. These divine aspects constitute the controlling factor and once they have gained possession of the sacred bull, the problem of Hercules is solved.

Keynotes of Taurus: "Let struggle be undismayed".

The Form Aspect.

"I see and when the Eye is opened, all is light".

The Soul Aspect.

from *Esoteric Astrology*, p. 403.

what does my soul desire
what does SHE desire
DO I NEED to Know?

Is that my problem, the
URGE to Know?

LABOUR III.

GATHERING THE GOLDEN APPLES OF THE HESPERIDES—PART I
(Gemini, May 21st-June 20th)

The Myth

The great Presiding One, within the Council Chamber of the Lord, had watched the labours of the son of man who is a son of God. He and the Teacher saw the third great Gate, opening before the son of man, revealing a new chance to tread the *Way*. They noted how the labourer arose and prepared to enter on his task.

"Send out the word to guard the sacred tree. Let Hercules unfold the power to search without discouragement, deception or too great a speed. Let perseverance now be called upon. He has done well so far". And thus the word went forth.

* * *

Far in a distant country grew the sacred tree, the tree of wisdom, and on it grew the golden apples of the Hesperides. The fame of these sweet fruits had gone to distant lands, and all the sons of men who knew themselves to be likewise the sons of God desired them. Hercules, too, knew of these fruits, and when the word went forth to seek for them he sought the Teacher, asking Him the way to go and find the sacred tree and pick the apples.

"Tell me the way, O Teacher of my soul. I seek the apples and I need them quickly for my use. Show me the quickest way and I will go!"

"Not so, my son", replied the Teacher, "the way is long. Two things alone I will confide to you, and then it is for you to prove the truth of what I say. Remember that the sacred tree is

54

guarded well. Three maidens fair cherish the tree, protecting well its fruit. A dragon with one hundred heads protects the maidens and the tree. Guard thyself well from strength too great for thee, from wiles too subtle for thy comprehension. Watch well. The second thing that I would say to thee is that thy search will carry thee where five great tests will meet thee on the *Way*. Each will afford thee scope for wisdom, understanding, skill and opportunity. Watch well. I fear, my son, that you will fail to recognise these points upon the *Way*. But time alone will show; God speed thee in thy search".

* * *

With confidence, because success nor failure held for him a claim, Hercules went forth upon the *Way*, sure of himself, his wisdom and his strength. Through the third Gate he passed, going due north. Throughout the land he passed, seeking the sacred tree, but found it not. All men he met he questioned, but none could guide him on his way; none knew the place. Time passed, yet still he sought, wandering from place to place and returning oft upon his steps to the third Gate. Sad and discouraged, still he sought on every hand.

The Teacher, watching from afar, sent Nereus to see if he could aid. Time and again he came, in varying form and with differing words of truth, but Hercules responded not, nor knew him for the messenger he was. Skilled though he was in speech and wise with the deep wisdom of a son of God, Nereus failed, for Hercules was blind. He did not recognise the help so subtly proffered. Returned at length with sadness to the Teacher, Nereus spoke of failure.

"The first of the five lesser tests is passed", replied the Teacher, "and failure marks this stage. Let Hercules proceed".

Finding no sacred tree upon the northern way, Hercules turned towards the south and in the place of darkness continued with his search. At first he dreamed of quick success, but Antaeus, the serpent, met him on that way and wrestled with him, overcoming him at every point.

"He guards the tree", said Hercules, "this I was told, so near him must be the tree. I must break down his guard and, thus destroying him, break down and pluck the fruit". Yet, wrestling with much strength, he conquered not.

"Where lies my fault?" said Hercules. "Why can Antaeus conquer me? E'en when an infant I destroyed a serpent in my cot. With my own hands I strangled it. Why fail I now?"

Wrestling again with all his might, he grasped the serpent with both hands, lifting it high in air, away from off the ground. And lo! the deed was done: Antaeus, vanquished, spoke: "I come again in different guise at the eighth Gate. Prepare again to wrestle".

The Teacher, gazing from afar, saw all that happened, and to the great Presiding One who sits within the Council Chamber of the Lord he spoke, reporting on the deed. "The second test is passed. The danger is surmounted. Success at this point marks his way". And the great Presiding One replied: "Let him proceed".

* * *

Happy and confident, Hercules went on, sure of himself and with new courage for the search. Now to the west he turned himself and, turning thus, he met disaster. He entered without thought upon the third great test and failure met him and for long delayed his steps.

For there he met Busiris, the great arch-deceiver, son of the waters, of close kin to Poseidon. His is the work to bring delusion to the sons of men through words of seeming wisdom. He claims to know the truth and with quickness they believe. He speaks fair words saying: "I am the teacher. To me is given knowledge of the truth and sacrifice for me.   Accept the way of life through me. I know, but no-one else. My truth is right. All other truth is wrong and false. Hark to my words; stay with me and be saved". And Hercules obeyed, and daily weakened

on the early way (third test) seeking no further f(
tree. His strength was sapped. He loved, adored ᴅᴜᴄ..
accepted all he said. Weaker from day to day he grew, until
there came a day when his loved teacher bound him to an altar
and kept him bound throughout a year.

Suddenly one day, when struggling to be free, and slowly
seeing Busiris for what he was, words spoken long ago by
Nereus came to his mind: "Truth lies within yourself.
There is a higher power and strength and wisdom in yourself.
Turn inwards and there evoke the strength which is, the
power which is the heritage of all the sons of men who are
the sons of God". Silent he lay a prisoner on the altar, bound
to its corners four for one whole year. Then, with the strength
which is the strength of all the sons of God, he broke his
bonds, seized the false teacher (who had seemed so wise) and
bound him to the altar in his place. He spoke no word, but
left him there to learn.

The watching Teacher, from afar, noted the moment of re-
lease, and turning to Nereus said: "The third great test is passed.
You taught him how to meet it and in due time he profited.
Let him go forward on the *Way* and learn the secret of success."

* * *

Chastened, yet full of questioning relief, Hercules continued with his search and wandered far. The year, spent prone
upon the altar, had taught him much. He went with greater wisdom on his way.

Suddenly, he halted in his steps. A cry of deep distress
smote on his ear. Some vultures circling o'er a distant rock
caught his attention; then again the cry broke forth. Should he
proceed upon his way, or should he seek the one who seemed
in need and thus retard his steps? He pondered on the problem
of delay; a year had now been lost; he felt the need for haste.
Again a cry broke forth and Hercules, with rapid steps, sped to

his brother's help. He found Prometheus chained upon a rock, suffering dire agonies of pain, caused by the vultures plucking at his liver, thus slowly killing him. He broke the binding chain and freed Prometheus, chasing the vultures to their distant lair, and tending the sick man until he had recovered from his wounds. Then, with much loss of time, he again started to make his way.

The Teacher, watching from afar, spoke to his seeking pupil these clear words, the first words spoken to him since he entered on his search: "The fourth stage on the way unto the sacred tree is passed. There has been no delay. The rule upon the chosen Path which hastens all success is, 'Learn to serve'."

The Presiding One, within the Council Chamber of the Lord, remarked: "He has done well. Continue with the tests".

* * *

He becomes a servant then BOOM Atlas.

Upon all ways the search went on, and north and south and east and west, the sacred tree was sought, but was not found. There came a day when, worn with fear and travelling, he heard a rumour from a passing pilgrim on the way that, near a distant mountain, the tree was to be found, the first true statement given him as yet. Therefore he turned his feet to the high mountains of the east and, on a bright and sunny day, he saw the object of his search and hastened then his steps. "Now I shall touch the sacred tree", he shouted in his joy, "surmount the guarding dragon; see the fair maidens of wide fame; and pluck the apples".

But again, he was arrested by a sense of deep distress. Atlas confronted him, staggering 'neath the load of worlds upon his back. His face was lined with suffering; his limbs were bowed with pain; his eyes were closed with agony; he asked no help; he saw not Hercules but stood bowed down with pain, with the weight of worlds. Hercules, trembling, watched and gauged the measure of the load and pain. He forgot about his

search. The sacred tree and apples faded from m.
sought to aid the giant and that without delay;
rushed and eagerly removed the load, lifting it of. ... shoulders of his brother onto his own back, shouldering the burden
of the worlds himself. He closed his eyes, bracing himself
with effort, and lo! the load rolled off, and he stood free, and
likewise Atlas.

Before him stood the giant and in his hand he held the
golden apples, offering them, with love, to Hercules. The search
was o'er.

The sisters three held still more golden apples, and pressed
them likewise into his hands, and Aegle, that fair maid who is
the glory of the setting sun, said unto him, placing an apple in
his hand, "The *Way* to us is always marked by service. Deeds
of love are signposts on the *Way*". Then Erytheia, who keeps
the gate which all must pass before they stand alone before the
great Presiding One, gave him an apple and upon its side, inscribed in light, was writ the golden word of *Service*. "Remember this", she said, "forget it not".

And lastly Hesperis came, the wonder of the evening star,
and said to him with clarity and love, "Go forth and serve, and
tread the way, from henceforth and for aye, of all world
servers."

"Then I give back these apples for those who follow on",
said Hercules, and returned from whence he came.

* * *

Before the Teacher then he stood and rendered due account
of all that had transpired. To him the Teacher gave the word of
cheer and then with pointing finger indicated the fourth Gate
and said to him: "Pass through that Gate. Capture the doe and
enter once again the Holy Place".

THE TIBETAN.

The Nature of the Test

We come now to the third labour, in the sign Gemini, concerning predominantly the active work of the aspirant on the physical plane as he comes to an understanding of himself. Before this active work becomes possible there must be a cycle of interior thought and mystical longing; the striving after the vision and a subjective process carried on, perhaps for a very long time, before the man on the physical plane really begins the labour of unifying soul and body. This is the theme of this labour. It is in this physical plane achievement, and in the work of gaining the golden apples of wisdom, that the real test of the sincerity of the aspirant takes place. A longing to be good, a deep desire to ascertain the facts of the spiritual life, spasmodic efforts at self-discipline, at prayer and meditation, precede, almost inevitably, this real and steady effort.

The visionary must become a man of action: desire has to be carried forward into the world of completion, and herein lies the test in Gemini. The physical plane is the place where experience is gained and where the causes, initiated in the world of mental effort, must manifest and achieve objectivity. It is the place also where the mechanism of contact is developed, where, little by little, the five senses open up to the human being new fields of awareness and present to him fresh spheres for conquest and achievement. It is the place, therefore, where knowledge is gained, and where that knowledge must be transmuted into wisdom. Knowledge, we know, is the quest of sense, whilst wisdom is the omniscience of the synthetic knowledge of the soul. Without understanding in the application of knowledge, however, we perish; for understanding is the application of knowledge in the light of wisdom to the problems of life, and to the attainment of the goal. In this labour, Hercules is faced with the tremendous task of bringing together the two poles of his being and of co-ordinating, or at-one-ing, soul and body, so that duality gives place to unity and the pairs of opposites are blended.

The Symbols

Eurystheus, having watched Hercules achieve mental control and then ride the bull of desire over into the Temple of the Soul, now sets him the task of fetching the golden apples from the garden of the Hesperides. The apple has long figured in mythology and in symbology. In the garden of Eden, as we know, the serpent gave the apple to Eve; and with the giving of that apple, and with its acceptance came the knowledge of good and of evil. This is a symbolic method of telling us the story of the appearance of mind, and of how it began to function in that early creature, which was neither animal nor strictly human. With the coming of mind came also the knowledge of duality, of the pull of the pairs of opposites, of the nature of the soul, which is good, and of the nature of the form, which is evil if it holds the soul and hinders it from full expression. It is not evil *per se*.

It is to be noted that in the garden of Eden one single apple was given to the human being, the symbol of separateness, isolation. Hercules had to hunt for the golden apples in another garden, and in the garden of the Hesperides the apples were the symbol of plurality, of synthesis, and of the many, nourished by the one tree of Life.

Hercules was told only three facts: that there was a garden containing a tree whereon grew the golden apples; that the tree was guarded by the hundred-headed serpent; that, when he found it, he would find there these three beautiful maidens. But in what direction lay the garden, and how to find it, he was not told. This time he was not confined to the wild lands, up and down which the man-eating mares ravaged; nor was he confined to the little island of Crete. The whole planet had to be searched, and he went up and down from north to south and from east to west, until at last he met Nereus, who was skilled in all wisdom and in all forms of speech. He is called in some of the classics, "the ancient of the sea". He was not only wise, but very elusive, assuming many forms, and refused ever to

give to Hercules a direct answer. Finally, he hinted as to the
direction in which the apples should be sought, sending him
on his way alone and somewhat discouraged, with only a
vague idea as to what he would have to do and where he
would have to go. All he knew was that he had to turn south;
a symbol of going back into the world, the opposite pole of
spirit.

He had no sooner done so than he met the serpent with
whom he had to wrestle.* In his search for the golden apples
on the physical plane, Hercules had to conquer, as do all disciples, glamour and illusion; for in the carrying forward of spiritual aspiration, the disciple is very apt to be taken in by
astralism and lower psychism in one form or another. As Hercules wrestled with the serpent, he found he could not overcome
it until he discovered that it was invincible only so long as it
was in contact with the earth. Just as soon as Hercules lifted the
serpent (Antaeus) high into the air, it became utterly weak and
unable to defeat him.

Gemini is an air sign, a mutable or common sign.
Glamour is ever changing, ever taking one form or another.
It concerns appearance and not reality, and the earth stands
for appearances.

Having vanquished the serpent that stood in his way, Hercules passed on in his search. His next encounter was with
glamour in another form. Busiris was a son of Poseidon, the
god of the waters, but his mother was a mere mortal. He
claimed to be a great teacher. He was fluent in speech and cap-
tivating in what he said. He made great claims for himself, leading Hercules to believe that he could show him the way, that he
could lead him out into the light, and that he was the custodian
of truth. Hercules was completely deceived. Little by little he
fell under the power and spell of Busiris; little by little he

---

*Known in mythology also as the giant, Antaeus, the son of Poseidon, god of
waters, and Gea, the earth. Hence when in touch with the earth, his mother,
he was invincible.

yielded up his will and his mind and accepted him as his teacher and guide. Finally, when Busiris had Hercules entirely under his control, he bound him to the altar of sacrifice and forced him to forget Nereus. The myth tells that Hercules eventually freed himself and resumed his search, binding Busiris to the altar whereon he himself had lain. Again we find discouragement, delay, failure and deceit characterising this part of the test.

Still searching up and down, he found Prometheus bound to a rock with the vultures tearing at his liver. The sight of such suffering was more than Hercules could bear and he turned aside from his search to release Prometheus, thus putting him in a position to drive away the vultures.

We come now to the crucial point of the Labour and to that which constituted the real test. Hercules finds Atlas bearing the load of the world on his shoulders, and staggering under the weight of the task he had undertaken. Hercules is so overcome by the stupendous enterprise of Atlas, and so concerned over his sufferings as he seeks to carry the weight of the world, that he gives up his search for the golden apples. He forgets what he himself has set out to do and, in pity, takes the load off the shoulders of Atlas and bears it himself. Then we are told, in the wonderful consummation of the story, that Atlas, freed from his burden, goes to the garden of the Hesperides, plucks the golden apples without any let or hindrance from the hundred-headed serpent, with the enthusiastic help of the three beautiful maidens, and brings the apples to Hercules, who now also stands free, in spite of all the obstacles and hindrances, the deviations due to glamour and illusion. Despite failures and the length of time it has taken him to arrive at wisdom, Hercules does obtain the golden apples. Note that the opposite, or consummating sign, of Gemini is that of Sagittarius, the Archer, who shoots straight and rides unhindered to the goal: no deviations, no failure! There is only a steady going forward.

LABOUR III.

GATHERING THE GOLDEN APPLES OF THE
HESPERIDES—PART 2
(Gemini, May 21st-June 20th)

The Field of the Labour

Gemini has in it two stars, called by the Greeks, Castor and Pollux, or the Twins. These personify two major groups of stars, the Seven Pleiades, and the Seven Stars of the Great Bear, which are the two constellations, in the north, around which our universe seems to revolve. One star represents each constellation. From the standpoint of esotericism, the great mystery of God incarnate in matter, and the crucifixion of the cosmic Christ upon the cross of matter, is tied up with the relationship (presumed from most ancient times to exist) between the stars of the Pleiades and those of the Great Bear. These two groups of stars represent God, the macrocosm, whilst in Gemini, Castor and Pollux were regarded as symbols of man, the microcosm. They were also called Apollo and Hercules: Apollo, meaning the Ruler, the Sun God; and Hercules, "the one who comes to labour". They represent, therefore, the two aspects of man's nature, the soul and the personality, the spiritual man and the human being through which that spiritual entity is functioning: Christ incarnate in matter, God working through form.

Castor was regarded as mortal and Pollux as immortal. It is an interesting astronomical fact that the star, Castor, is waning in brilliancy and has not the light that it had several hundred years ago; whilst Pollux, the immortal brother, is waxing in brightness and eclipsing his brother, so reminding one of the words of John the Baptist, spoken as he looked at the Christ, "He must increase, but I must decrease". (*St. John,* III, 30) Thus we have a most significant constellation, because it holds always before the eyes of man the thought of the increasing potency of the spiritual life and the decreasing power of the personal self. The story of man's growth to maturity and the history of the soul's gradually increasing control are told for us in the constellation Gemini.

In the ancient zodiac of Denderah, this sign is called "the place of Him who cometh", and the thought of an emerging spiritual Being is held before us. It is represented by two figures, the one male, the other female; one, the positive, spirit aspect, and the other, the negative, matter aspect. The Coptic and the Hebrew names signify "united", and this is the status of Hercules, the aspirant. He is soul and body unified. This was the problem to be wrestled with in the sign Gemini. The at-one-ment of the lower with the higher self, of the mortal and the immortal aspects, is the objective. It was this problem that created the devious and prolonged search that Hercules undertook, for he was at length attentive to the voice of Nereus, the higher self, but sometimes under the illusion and glamour of the lower self.

The duality which is emphasised in Gemini runs through a large number of the mythological stories. We meet the same brothers again in Romulus and Remus, for instance, and in Cain and Abel, one brother dying and the other living. We meet the astrological symbol for Gemini in the two pillars of Masonry, and many believe that the Masonic tradition could, if we had the power to do so, be traced back to that period, ante-dating the Taurian age, when the sun was in Gemini, and to that great cycle in which the Lemurian race, the first strictly human race, came into being; where the mind aspect began to emerge, and the duality of mankind became a fact in nature.

The Lemurian race was the third race; and this labour that Hercules symbolically undertook, is the third labour. The search upon which he was engaged was for the soul, and this has ever been the unrecognised search of the human being until the time comes when he knows himself to be Hercules and starts to concentrate upon the search for the golden apples of instruction and wisdom. So we have in the Masonic tradition the search of the human family typified, the search for light, the search for unity, the search for divinity. And so the two pillars, Boaz and Jachin, stand as the emblems of that duality.

In China, Castor and Pollux are spoken of as the two "gods of the door", showing the tremendous power that the god of matter can assume, and also the potency of divinity.

Gemini is predominantly the sign of the intellect and it has a peculiarly vital effect in our Aryan race. In this race the mind faculty and the intellect have been steadily developed. Gemini, therefore, has influence in three departments, which concern themselves with human relations. First, it governs all education. It deals with knowledge, with the sciences, and lays the foundation for wisdom. One educator has said that "the ultimate purpose of education is the acquiring of knowledge in order to receive the higher revelation. The unintelligent may receive it, but they cannot interpret it". In this labour, Hercules receives an outstanding revelation and in the five stages of his search his education is steadily carried forward.

The exoteric ruler of Gemini and of the first decanate is Mercury for, as Alan Leo tells us:

"Mercury in the outer world signifies schools, colleges, and all places where teaching and learning go on, scientific and literary institutions...In consciousness, it signifies thought, understanding, reason, intelligence, intellect; the abstract kinds rather than the concrete, knowledge for its own sake...Its highest application seems to be what is called 'pure reason'...In body, it governs the brain and nervous system, the tongue and organs of speech, the hands as instruments of intelligence". (Alan Leo, *Complete Dictionary of Astrology,* p. 163)

Gemini stands, secondly, for the relation between. It governs, therefore, language, intercourse or intercommunication and commerce. It is interesting to note that the United States

and London are both governed by Gemini; that th
language is becoming predominantly the world tongue; that
the greatest lines of ocean communication start from New
York or London, and that both these cities have been world
markets and world centres of distribution. Mercury, the ruling
planet of the sign, is the interpreter, the messenger of the
gods. It is worth noticing also in this connection how Hercules comes under the influence of two teachers: Nereus, the
higher teacher, and Busiris, the lower or psychic teacher; and
thus we again have emphasised both the duality of Gemini
and its mental quality.

When this sign is in evidence as it is now, being a powerful
mutable sign, it inaugurates many changes; new ideas flood the
world; new impulses make their presence felt; new and undeveloped lines of approach to spiritual truth emerge, and many
teachers will arise everywhere to help lead the race into a new
state of spiritual awareness. Being an air sign, we find that the
conquest of the air proceeds with speed, and also a constant effort is made to unify and co-ordinate the many and varied aspects of human endeavour.

Venus is the esoteric ruler of Gemini and governs the second decanate; for Venus makes at-one, and through its influence the law of attraction and the bringing together of the polar
opposites takes place. But all these changes and unifications
naturally inaugurate a new state of awareness, a new state of
being, and bring in a new age and a new world. Consequently,
new difficulties and problems arise and we find Saturn governing the last decanate, for Saturn is the planet of discipleship; the planet that brings about the difficulties, problems and
tests that offer to the disciple immediate opportunity. It is Saturn that opens the door into incarnation, and Saturn that opens
the door on to the path of initiation. Mercury, the interpreter,
and the illuminating intellect; Venus, the principle of attraction
and of at-one-ment; and Saturn, the generator of opportunity:
these three play their parts in the life of the aspirant as he uni-

fies higher and lower, passes through the five stages in this test, and visions the goal which ultimately he must achieve.

The Three Symbolic Constellations

The three constellations to be found in connection with the sign are Lepus, the Hare, Canis Major and Canis Minor, and in their interrelation and in their association with Hercules, the aspirant, the whole story of the human being is again most strikingly portrayed. In Canis Major we find Sirius, the Dog Star, called in many old books "the leader of the entire heavenly host", for it is ten or twelve times brighter than any other star of the first magnitude. Sirius has always been associated with great heat, hence we have the phrase of "the dog days" in the middle of the summer, when the heat is supposed to be greatest. From the standpoint of the occultist, Sirius is of profound significance. "Our God is a consuming fire", and Sirius is the symbol of the universal soul as well as of the individual soul. It is therefore, esoterically considered, the star of initiation. In the language of symbology we are told, there comes a moment when a star blazes forth before the initiate, signifying his realisation of his identity with the universal soul, and this he suddenly glimpses through the medium of his own soul, his own star.

Canis Major is the immortal Hound of Heaven, that chases forever the lesser Dog, the underdog, the man in physical incarnation. This chase has been immortalised for us by Francis Thompson in *The Hound of Heaven.*

"I fled Him, down the nights and down the days;
I fled Him, down the arches of the years;
I fled Him, down the labyrinthine ways
Of my own mind; and in the mist of tears
I hid from Him, and under running laughter.
    Up vistaed hopes I sped;
    And shot, precipitated,
Adown Titanic glooms of chasmed fears,
    From those strong feet that followed, followed after".

In the zodiac of Denderah, this star is called Apes, the head. We are told (in the appendix, p. 1518, of the *Companion Bible*) that the brightest star in Canis Major is Sirius, the Prince, called in Persian, the Chieftain. There are three other stars in the same constellation: one is called "the announcer", another the "shining one", and the third, "the glorious", all of them phrases emphasising the magnificence of Canis Major and, esoterically, the wonder and the glory of the higher self.

In Canis Minor, the "underdog", the same writing tells us that the name of the brightest star signifies, "redeemer", that the next brightest is "the burden bearer" or "the one who bears for others". We have, therefore, in the significance of these two names, a portrayal of Hercules, as he works out his own salvation and as he bears the great burden of Atlas and learns the meaning of service.

Lepus, the Hare, associated with these two constellations, contains a star of the most intense crimson colour, almost like a drop of blood. Red is ever the symbol of desire for material things. In the zodiac of Denderah, the name given is Bashtibeki, which means "falling confounded". Aratus, writing about 250 B.C., speaks of Lepus as being "chased eternally", and it is interesting to note that the Hebrew names of some of the stars found in this constellation signify "the enemy of the Coming One", which is the meaning of the name of the brightest star, Arneb; whilst three other stars have names meaning "the mad", "the bound", "the deceiver". All these words are characteristics of the lower self chased eternally by the higher self; the human soul pursued by the Hound of Heaven.

As we look at the starry heavens at night and locate Sirius, the Dog Star, the story of our past, present and future is dramatically pictured. We have the story of our *past* in Lepus, the Hare, fleet of foot, deceived, mad, bound to the wheel of life, identified with the matter aspect, and ever the enemy of "The Coming Prince". In Canis Minor, we have the story of the aspirant, of our *present* lot. Dwelling within us is the inner ruler, the hidden divinity, the redeemer. We go forth conquering and to conquer, but we have to do it as the burdened disciple, bearing for others and serving. In Canis Major we have portrayed our *future* and a consummation, glorious beyond all present realisation. Were all religions and all scriptures of the world to be lost, and were there nothing left to us except the starry heavens, the story of the zodiac and the significance of the names of the various stars found in the different constellations, we should be able to retrace the history of man, recover the knowledge of our goal and learn the mode of its achievement.

illusion → fix your why

The Lesson of the Labour

The whole of this story really signifies the lesson which is the first that all aspirants have to master, and one which it is impossible to learn until the tests in Aries and in Taurus have been undergone. Then, on the physical plane, in the field of the brain and in his waking consciousness, the disciple has to register contact with the soul and to recognise its qualities. He must no longer be the visionary mystic, but must add to the mystical achievement the occult knowledge of reality. This is often forgotten by aspirants. They rest content with aspiration and with the vision of the heavenly goal. They have wrought out in the crucible of life an equipment that is characterised by sincerity, good desire, fine character, and they are conscious of purity of motive, a willingness to fulfil the requirements, and the satisfaction that they have reached a certain status of development which entitles them to go on. But one thing still lacks: they have not what might be called "technique of the presence;" they have not privilege and prerogative to possess. They believe in the fact of the soul, in the possibility of perfection, in the path which must be trodden; but belief has not yet been transmuted into knowledge of the spiritual realm and they know not how to make their goal! So they, as Hercules did, start on the five-fold search.

The first stage of that search is full of encouragement for them, had they been able to recognise the happening. Like Hercules, they meet Nereus, the symbol of the higher self, and, later on in the history of the disciple, he is the symbol of the teaching Master. When contacted, especially in the early stages of the search, the higher self will manifest as a flash of illumination, and lo! it is gone; as a sudden realisation of truth, so elusive, so fleeting, that at first the disciple cannot grasp it; as a hint dropped into the consciousness in moments of one-pointed attention, when the mind is held steady and the emotions temporarily cease to control.

In the case of a more advanced disciple who has established contact with his soul and who, therefore, may be supposed to be ready for instruction from one of the great Teachers of the Race, it will be found that the Master works just as Nereus did. He cannot always be contacted, and only occasionally does the disciple come into touch with him. When he does, he need not expect congratulations upon his wonderful progress, nor will he find a careful elucidation of his problem, nor a lengthy outline of the work that he should do. The Master will give a hint and disappear. He will make a suggestion and will say no more. It is for the disciple to act upon the hint as best he may and to follow up the suggestion should he deem it wise.

Many well-meaning occultists would lead one to believe that the Masters of the Wisdom take a personal interest in them, that the overburdened Guides of the Race have no better occupation than to tell them personally how to live, how to solve their problems and how, in detail, to guide their undertakings. I would like here to go on record as protesting against any such belittling of the work of the Great Ones. The reasons that Nereus, the Master, is elusive and gives but a flash of thought or of momentary attention to the aspirant, are two:

First, the individual aspirant is of no personal interest to the Master until he has achieved the point in his evolution where he is so closely in touch with his soul that he becomes a magnetic server in the world. Then, and then only, will it profit the Master to throw him a thought, and to give him a hint. Then, as those hints are followed, he may give him more, but, and this is the point that must be emphasised, *only in connection with the work that he has to do in the field of world service.* Aspirants need to remember that they become masters only by mastering, and that we are taught to be masters and are brought to the position of membership in the band of world servers through the efforts of our own soul. That soul is a divine son of God, omniscient and omnipotent. As the immortal twin increases in power and brilliance, that of the mortal brother decreases.

Second, the physical bodies of the aspirants are in no condition to stand the greatly heightened vibration of One who has achieved. The body would be shattered and the brain overstrained if one of the Masters made constant contact with a disciple before he had even learned to know Nereus as the symbol of his own higher self. When by our own efforts we are beginning to live as souls, and when by our own self-initiated endeavour we are learning to serve and be channels of spiritual energy, then we shall know Nereus more intimately; and then, almost inevitably, our knowledge of the work that the Great Ones have to do will be so vital and so real that we will forego our own desire for contact and seek only to lift the burden that They carry.

At the beginning of his search, Hercules met Nereus; but he was not impressed and so wandered elsewhere, furiously seeking the satisfaction of his aspiration. At the close of his search he meets Atlas, bearing the burden of the world, and so impressed is he with the weight of that responsibility and the load that Atlas, the great Master, is carrying, that he forgets all about the goal and his search for the golden apples and endeavours to lift the burden off the shoulders of Atlas. When aspirants in the religious field and in the Church, in the Theosophical field, in the Rosicrucian field, and in the many groups to which they gravitate, have learned to forget themselves in service and to lose sight of their spiritual selfishness by helping humanity, there will be a much more rapid gathering in of initiates through the portal on to the Path that leads from darkness to the Light, and from the unreal to the Real. One of the Great Ones has said that "there are persons, who, without ever having any external sign of selfishness, are intensely selfish in their inner spiritual aspiration". (p. 360, *The Mahatma Letters to A.P Sinnett*). And later he holds out before us a stupendous ideal which cuts at the root of spiritual selfishness: "In our view the highest aspirations for the welfare of humanity become tainted with selfishness if, in the mind of the philanthropist, there lurks the shadow of desire for self-benefit. . .".

Hercules, the disciple, has known the touch of the higher self, but he did not know enough to stay with Nereus. So he turns south, or back into the world. He has had his high moment, when he transcended his brain consciousness and held converse with his soul. But this does not last, and he drops back into the brain consciousness and enters upon another experience. He has to wrestle with Antaeus, the serpent (or giant). But, this time, it is the serpent of astral glamour and not primarily the serpent of desire. It is with the glamours of lower psychism that he has to wrestle, and these seem, in the early stages, inevitably to attract the interest of aspirants. Any teacher who has worked with those who are seeking the Way knows the glamour under which they can so easily fall. According to the temperament of the aspirant so will be the glamour. Some get side-tracked by spiritualistic phenomena. In the endeavour to penetrate within the veil, they become engrossed with the lower side of spiritualism and pass much time in the seance room studying over and over again the same old phenomena of materialisation, spirit communication and manifestations. I make here no reference to the truly scientific investigations of those who go deeply into this research, and who are equipped so to do. I refer to the ignorant participation in certain types of seance room work. This intrigues the average man or woman and puts them at the mercy of the equally ignorant medium or the charlatan, for they are unequipped to verify in any way that which they see and hear.

The serpent may take the form of the more common aspect of psychic phenomena. The aspirant becomes interested in automatic writing, or he learns to sit and listen to "voices", he becomes astrally clairvoyant or clairaudient, and adds to the confusion of the physical plane and his own particular environment, the still greater confusion of the psychic plane, and so falls into the snares and pitfalls of astralism. He becomes negative, because he is all the time trying to hear or see that which is not physical. Because we share with cats and dogs the capacity to be clairvoyant and clairaudient, in due time we shall surely see or hear, if not in truth, yet through the power of that creative faculty which we all possess, a creative imagination. But in some form or another, the aspirant who has left Nereus will meet the serpent and will have to wrestle with him. As the myth states, for a long time Hercules could not conquer, but when he lifted the serpent high up into the air, he prevailed.

There is a great truth underlying this symbolism. The air has always been regarded as the symbol or the element related to the Christ plane, called in the Theosophical terminology and in the east, the buddhic plane. The astral plane is the distorted reflection of the buddhic plane, and it is only when we carry glamour up into the clear light of the Christ soul that we shall see truth as it is, and become invincible. Most solemnly, I would urge upon all aspirants to forego all interest in psychic phenomena, and to shut out as steadily as they can the astral plane until they have developed the power to be intuitive and to interpret their intuitions through the medium of a well-developed, well-stocked, well-trained mind.

The next stage of the search of Hercules is equally applicable to humanity as a whole. He fell into the clutches of Busiris, who claimed to be a great teacher. For a long period of time Hercules was kept in bondage. The world today is full of teachers, and like Busiris, they base their teaching upon portentous claims; they claim to be initiates, to be the custodians of truth, and to have a sure and certain way of development which must inevitably enable the aspirant to achieve. They bolster up their position by promises; they build up a strong personality relationship, and by utilising the sincerity and the aspiration of the seeker after truth, they gather around themselves groups of men and women who innocently and sincerely believe the truth of the claims that they make, and bind them to the altar of sacrifice for a longer or a shorter period of time. The true initiate is known by his life and acts, he is too busy serving the race to find the time to interest people in himself, and he cannot make promises beyond saying to every aspirant: "These are the ancient rules, this is the way that all the saints and Masters of the Wisdom have trod, this is the discipline to which you must subject yourself; and if you will but try and have endurance and patience, the goal will surely be yours".

But Hercules freed himself, as do all sincere seekers; and having escaped from the world of psychic and pseudo-spiritual glamour, he began to serve. First he freed himself under the symbol of Prometheus, who signifies God incarnate, releasing him from the torture of the vultures of old. The solar plexus, the stomach and the liver are externalisations, if I might so express it, of the desire nature, and Hercules freed himself from the vultures of desire that had for so long tortured him. He gave up being selfish, and gave up satisfying himself. He had had two bitter lessons in this sign and *for this particular cycle* was relatively free. Prometheus, the God within, could go forward to the service of the world and to lifting the burden of Atlas.

After the sacrifice comes the reward, and Hercules received his great surprise after freeing both Prometheus and Atlas. Having given up his search in order to help the world, Atlas went for him to the garden and handed to him the golden apples, bringing him in touch with the three beautiful maidens, the three aspects of the soul.

At the beginning of this labour he contacts his soul as Nereus; at the close of this labour, having overcome much glamour, he achieves a greatly increased vision of his soul and sees it in its three aspects, each one holding in it the potency of the three principles of divinity. Aegle symbolises the glory of the life and the splendour of the setting sun; the magnificence of manifestation on the physical plane. She gives an apple to Hercules, saying, "The way to us is ever through deeds of love". Erytheia keeps the gate, the soul, which is ever opened by Love-Wisdom, and she gives to Hercules an apple marked with the golden word *Service*. Hesperis, the evening star, the star of initiation, typifies the Will. She says to Hercules, "Tread the Way". Body, soul and spirit; Intelligence, Love and Will, visioned and contacted by the selfless aspirant through *Service*.

LABOUR IV.

THE CAPTURE OF THE DOE OR HIND—PART I
(Cancer, June 21st-July 21st)

The Myth

The great Presiding One, who sits within the Council Chamber of the Lord, spoke to the Teacher, standing by his side: "Where is the son of man who is the son of God? How fares he? How is he tested and with what service is he now engaged?"

The Teacher said, casting his eye upon the son of man who is a son of God: "Naught at this time, O great Presiding One. The third great test provided much of teaching sustenance to a learner such as he. He ponders and reflects".

"Provide a test which will evoke his wisest choice. Send him to labour in a field wherein he must decide which voice, of all the many voices, will arouse the obedience of his heart. Provide likewise a test of great simplicity upon the outer plane, and yet a test which will awaken, on the inner side of life, the fulness of his wisdom and the rightness of his power to choose. Let him proceed with the fourth test".

* * *

Before the fourth great Gate stood Hercules; a son of man and yet a son of God. At first was silence deep. He uttered not a word or made a sound. Beyond the Gate the landscape stretched in contours fair and on the far horizon stood the temple of the Lord, the shrine of the Sun-God, the gleaming battlements. Upon a hill nearby there stood a slender fawn. And Hercules, who is a son of man and yet a son of God, both watched and listened and, listening, heard a voice. The voice

77

came out from that bright circle of the moon which is the home of Artemis. And Artemis, the fair, spoke words of warning to the son of man.

"The doe is mine, so touch it not", she said. "For ages long I nurtured it and tended it when young. The doe is mine and mine it must remain."

Then into view Diana sprang, the huntress of the heavens, the daughter of the sun. Leaping on sandalled feet towards the doe, she likewise claimed possession.

"Not so", she said, "Artemis, fairest maid; the doe is mine and mine it must remain. Too young until today, it now can be of use. The golden antlered hind is mine, not yours, and mine it shall remain".

Hercules, standing between the pillars of the Gate, listened and heard the quarrel, and wondered much as the two maidens strove for possession of the doe.

Another voice fell on his ear, and with commanding accents said: "The doe belongs to neither maid, O Hercules, but to the God whose shrine you see on yonder distant mount. Go rescue it and bear it to the safety of the shrine, and leave it there. A simple thing to do, O son of man, yet (and ponder well my words) being a son of God, you thus can seek and hold the doe. Go forth".

* * *

Through the fourth Gate sprang Hercules, leaving behind the many gifts received and cumbered not himself in the swift chase which lay ahead. And from a distance the quarrelling maidens watched. Artemis, the fair, bending from out the moon and Diana, beauteous huntress of the woods of God, followed the movements of the doe and, when due cause arose, they each deluded Hercules, seeking to foil his efforts. He chased the doe from point to point and each with subtlety deceived him. And this they did, time and again.

Thus for the length of a full year, the son of man who is a son of God followed the doe from place to place, catching swift glimpses of its form, only to find that in the fastness of the deep woods it had been lost. From hill to hill and wood to wood, he hunted it until close to a quiet pool, full-length upon the untrampled grass, he saw it sleeping, wearied with its flight.

With quiet step, outstretched hand and steadfast eye, he shot an arrow towards the doe and in its foot he wounded it. Exciting all the will of which he was possessed, he nearer drew and yet the doe moved not. Thus he drew close, and clasped the doe within his arms, close to his heart. And Artemis and fair Diana both looked on.

"The search is o'er", he chanted loud. "Into the northern darkness I was led, and found no doe. Into the deep dark woods I fought my way, but found no doe; and over dreary plains and arid wilderness and deserts wild, I struggled towards the doe, yet found it not. At each point reached, the maidens turned my steps, but still I did persist and now the doe is mine! the doe is mine!"

"Not so, O Hercules", came to his ears the voice of one who stands close to the great Presiding One within the Council Chamber of the Lord. "The doe belongs not to a son of man, e'en though a son of God. Carry the doe to yonder distant shrine, where dwell the sons of God and leave it there with them".

"Why so, O Teacher wise? The doe is mine; mine by long search and travel, and mine likewise because I hold the doe close to my heart".

"And are you not a son of God, although a son of man? And is the shrine not also your abode? And share you not the life of all who dwell therein? Bear to the shrine of God the sacred doe, and leave it there, O son of God".

* * *

Then to the holy shrine of Mykenae, Hercules bore the doe, carrying it to the centre of the holy place and there he laid it down. And as he laid it down before the Lord, he noted on its foot the wound, made by an arrow from the bow he had possessed and used. The doe was his by right of search. The doe was his by right of skill and the prowess of his arm. "The doe is therefore doubly mine", he said.

But Artemis, standing within the outer court of that most holy place heard his loud cry of victory and said: "Not so. The doe is mine and always has been mine. I saw its form, reflected in the water; I heard its feet upon the ways of earth; I know the doe is mine, for every form is mine".

The Sun-God spoke, from out the holy place. "The doe is mine, not yours, O Artemis! Its spirit rests with me from all eternity, here in the centre of the holy shrine. You may not enter here, O Artemis, but know I speak the truth. Diana, that fair huntress of the Lord, may enter for a moment and tell you what she sees".

Into the shrine for one brief moment passed the huntress of the Lord and saw the form of that which was the doe, lying before the altar, seeming dead. And in distress she said: "But if its spirit rests with thee, O great Apollo, noble son of God, then know the doe is dead. The doe is slain by the man who is a son of man, e'en though a son of God. Why may he pass within the shrine and we await the doe out here?"

"Because he bore the doe within his arms, close to his heart, and in the holy place the doe finds rest, and so does man. All men are mine. The doe is likewise mine, not yours, nor man's but mine".

* * *

And Hercules, returning from the test, passed through the Gate again and found his way, back to the teacher of his life.

"I have fulfilled the task, set by the great Presiding One. Simple it was, except for length of time and wariness of search. I listened not to those who made their claim, nor faltered on the Way. The doe is in the holy place, close to the heart of God and likewise, in the hour of need, close to my heart also.

"Go look again, O Hercules, my son, between the pillars of the Gate". And Hercules obeyed. Beyond the Gate, the landscape stretched in contours fair and on the far horizon stood the temple of the Lord, the shrine of the Sun-God, with glistening battlements, whilst on a nearby hill there stood a slender fawn.

"Did I perform the test, O Teacher wise? The fawn is back upon the hill where I earlier saw it stand".

And from the Council Chamber of the Lord, where sits the great Presiding One, there came a voice: "Again and yet again must all the sons of men, who are the sons of God, seek for the golden antlered fawn and bear it to the holy place; again and yet again".

Then said the Teacher to the son of man who is a son of God: "Labour the fourth is over, and from the nature of the test and from the nature of the doe, frequent must be the search. Forget this not, but ponder on the lesson learnt".

THE TIBETAN.

Synthesis of the Signs

Cancer is the last of what we might call the four preparatory signs, whether we are considering the involution of the soul in matter, or the evolution of the aspirant as he struggles out of the human into the spiritual Kingdom. Being equipped with the faculty of mind, in Aries, and with desire, in Taurus, and having arrived at the realisation of his essential duality, in Gemini, the incarnating human being enters, through birth in Cancer, into the human kingdom.

Cancer is a mass sign, and the influences which pour from it are held by many esotericists to bring about the formation of the human family, of the race, the nation, and the family unit. Where the aspirant is concerned, the story is somewhat different, for in these four signs, he prepares his equipment and learns to utilise it. In Aries, he grips his mind and seeks to bend it to his need, learning mental control. In Taurus, "the mother of illumination", he receives his first flash of that spiritual light which will grow increasingly more brilliant as he nears his goal. In Gemini, he not only appreciates the two aspects of his nature, but the immortal aspect begins to increase at the expense of the mortal.

Now, in Cancer, he gets his first touch of that more universal sense which is the higher aspect of the mass consciousness. Equipped, therefore, with a controlled mind, a capacity to register illumination, an ability to contact his immortal aspect and intuitively to recognise the kingdom of spirit, he is ready now for the greater work.

In the next four signs, which we might regard as the signs of physical plane struggle for achievement, we have portrayed for us the tremendous battle through the medium of which the Self-conscious individual, emerging out of the mass in Cancer, knows himself to be the individual in Leo, the potential Christ in Virgo, the aspirant endeavouring to balance the pairs of opposites in Libra, and the one who overcomes illusion, in Scorpio. These are the four signs of crisis and of stupendous endeavour. In them all the illumination, intuition and soul power of which Hercules, the aspirant, is capable, are utilised to the uttermost. These have their reflection, too, on the involutionary arc, and a similar sequence of unfoldment can be traced. The soul achieves individuality in Leo, becomes the nurturer of ideas and of potential capacities in Virgo, swings violently from one extreme to the other in Libra, and is subjected to the disciplining effect of the world of illusion and form in Scorpio.

In the final four signs, we have the signs of achievement. The aspirant has worked out of the world of glamour and of form, and in his consciousness is free from their limitations. Now he can be the archer in Sagittarius, going straight for his goal; now he can be the goat in Capricorn, scaling the mount of initiation; now he can be the world worker in Aquarius, and the world saviour in Pisces. Thus he can sum up in himself all the gains of the preparatory period and of the fiercely fought battles in the four signs of strenuous activity; and in these four final signs demonstrate the gains achieved and the powers developed.

This brief summation of the signs, as they affect Hercules, will serve to give some idea of the wonderful synthesis of the picture, and of the steady progression, and of the controlled unfolding of the various forces which play their subtle parts in bringing about the changes in the life of man.

Three words summarise the objective self-awareness or the conscious aspect of the evolving human being: instinct, intellect, intuition. The sign which we are now studying is predominantly the sign of instinct; but the sublimation of instinct is the intuition. In the same way, as matter has to be lifted up into heaven, so instinct has to be likewise lifted up, and when it has been thus transcended and transmuted, it manifests as intuition (symbolised by the doe). The intermediate stage is that of the intellect. The great need of Hercules now is to develop his intuition and to become familiar with that instantaneous recognition of truth and reality which is the high prerogative and potent factor in the life of a liberated son of God.

Meaning of the Story

Eurystheus, therefore, sent Hercules to capture the golden horned Keryneian doe or hind. The word "hind" comes from an old Gothic word, meaning "that which must be seized", in other words, that which is elusive and difficult to secure. This doe was sacred to Artemis, the goddess of the moon; but Diana, the huntress of the heavens, the daughter of the sun, also claimed it and there was a quarrel as to ownership. Hercules accepted the charge of Eurystheus and set out to capture the gentle hind. He was a whole year hunting it, going from one forest to another, just catching sight of it and then again losing

ıfter month went by, and he never could catch and
...ıu ıt. Success at last crowned his efforts and he seized the
doe, flung it over his shoulder, "held it close to his heart", and
carried it to the sacred temple at Mykenae, where he laid it
down before the altar, in the holy place. Then he stood back,
pleased with his success.

This is one of the shortest of the stories but though we are
told very little, this labour, when considered thoughtfully, is one
of profound and outstanding interest and the lesson it holds is
of deep import. There is no success for the aspirant until he has
transmuted instinct into intuition, nor is there right use of the
intellect until the intuition is brought into play, interpreting and
extending the intellect and bringing realisation. Then instinct
is subordinated to both.

LABOUR IV.

THE CAPTURE OF THE DOE OR HIND—PART II
(Cancer, June 21st-July 21st)

Qualities of the Sign

Cancer is called the Crab and the Greeks tell us that it was the crab that was sent by Hera to bite the foot of Hercules. (Again we meet this symbol in the vulnerable "heel of Achilles".) This is an interesting way of expressing the liabilities of the incarnation process and of illustrating the handicaps which beset the soul as it travels along the path of evolution. It symbolises the limitations of all physical incarnation, for Cancer is one of the two great gates of the zodiac. It is the gate into the world of forms, into physical incarnation, and the sign wherein the duality of form and of soul is unified in the physical body.

The opposite sign to Cancer is Capricorn, and these two constitute the two gates, one being the gate into form life, and the other into spiritual life; one opening the door into the mass form of the human family, and the other into the universal state of consciousness, which is the kingdom of spirit. One marks the beginning of human experience on the physical plane, the other marks its climax. One signifies potentiality, and the other consummation.

We are told that Christ gave to Saint Peter the keys of heaven and earth; He gave to him, therefore, the keys of these two gates. We read:

"Jesus gives to Peter...the keys to the two principal gates of the zodiac, which are the two solsticial points, the zodiacal signs Cancer and Capricorn, called the gates of the sun. Through Cancer, or the 'gate of man,' the soul descends upon earth (to unite with the body), which is its spiritual death. Through Capricorn, the 'gate of the gods,' it reascends to heaven". (E. Valentia Straiton, *The Celestial Ship of the North*, Vol. II, p. 206).

In the zodiac of Denderah, the sign Cancer is represented by a beetle, called in Egypt, the scarab. The word "scarab" means "only begotten"; it stands, therefore, for birth into incarnation, or, in relation to the aspirant, for the new birth. The month of June, in ancient Egypt was called "meore", which again means "rebirth", and thus both the sign and the name hold steadily before us the thought of the taking of form and of coming into physical incarnation. In an ancient zodiac in India, dated about 400 B.C., the sign is represented again by a beetle.

The Chinese called this sign "the red bird", for red is the symbol of desire, and the bird is the symbol of that flashing forth into incarnation and of appearance in time and space. The bird appears quite frequently in the zodiac and in ancient mythological stories, *Hamsa,* the bird of the Hindu tradition, "the bird out of time and space", stands equally for the manifestation of God and of man. Out of the darkness flashes the bird and flies across the horizon in the light of the day, disappearing again into the darkness. Our word, "goose", comes from the same Sanskrit root, through the Icelandic, and when we say, "What a goose you are", we are really making a most esoteric affirmation; we are saying to another human being: "You are the bird out of time and space, you are the soul taking form; you are God in incarnation!"

The crab lives half on the earth, and half in the water. It is the sign, therefore, of the soul dwelling in the physical body, but predominantly living in the water, which is the symbol of the emotional, feeling nature.

Exoterically Cancer is ruled by the moon, which is always the mother of form, controlling the waters and the tides. Therefore, in this sign the form is dominant, and constitutes a handicap. The crab builds its house or shell and carries it upon its hack, and people born in this sign are always conscious of that which they have built; they are usually over-sensitive, over-emotional, ever seeking to hide away. The Cancer native is so sensitive that he is difficult to handle and so elusive and sometimes so indefinite, that it is hard to understand him or to pin him down.

The Cardinal Cross

Cancer is one of the arms of the cardinal cross. One arm is Aries, the sign of beginning, of commencement, of subjective life, of the prenatal stage, or involution, and of the first step, either towards form-taking, or towards spiritual liberation. A third arm of the cross is Libra, the balance, the choosing between, the beginning of the treading of the "narrow razor-edged path", to which the Buddha so frequently refers. Capricorn, the fourth arm, again is birth, the birth of the world saviour, birth into the spiritual kingdom, birth out of the world of matter into the world of being. Involution, incarnation, expression, inspiration, are the four words that express the story of the cardinal cross in the heavens. (The cross of the initiate.)

The Stars

There are no bright stars at all in Cancer, no conspicuous or brilliant star, because Cancer is a sign of hiding, of retreat behind that which has been constructed. It is not a striking constellation. It is interesting to note that there is no Hebrew word for "crab". It was regarded as unclean and not mentioned. So is the material form regarded from the standpoint of spirit, and esotericists tell us that the physical body is not a principle. (The substitution of the Egyptian sacred scarab for the crab seems a recognition of the quality of Cancer in its higher aspects when the native is an aspirant or disciple, for we go round the zodiac many times.)

There are eighty-three stars in this sign, the brightest of which is of the third magnitude, and in the very centre of the constellation there is a cluster of stars; Praesepe, the manger called by modern astronomers, "the beehive". The latter is a marvellous symbol of the collective organisation of the human family, and is one of the reasons why this is always regarded as a mass sign. In the mass, instinct rules; therefore, Cancer is the sign of instinct, of herd life, of mass reaction. It represents the subconscious mind, hereditary instinct, and the collective imagination. It stands, individually, for the totality of the life and the consciousness of the cells in the body, and of that instinctive, collective life, which is largely subconscious in man, but which always influences his physical body and, subjectively, his lower mind and emotional being.

The unevolved Cancer native is immersed in the mass; he is an unconscious part of the great whole, and therein lies the problem; for the average Cancer person, as well as for the aspirant who is performing the labour of this sign, is subjected to the urge to lift himself up out of the mass to which he is held by his instinct, and to develop instead the intuition, which will enable him so to rise. This sign is sometimes called "the coffin", by the Hebrews, because it marks loss of identity, whilst the early Christians called it "the grave of Lazarus", who was raised from the dead. In these words, "coffin", "grave", "crab", and in the reference which we sometimes find to Cancer as "the womb", we have the thought of hidden life, of a veiling form, of potentiality, and of that struggle with circumstances which will eventually produce, in Leo, the emergence of the individual and, in Capricorn, the birth of a world saviour. Definitely, therefore, it portrays the struggle that goes on in the life of the aspirant so that instinct can give place eventually to intuition.

At-one-ment with Capricorn

It is interesting to contrast the two signs, Cancer and Capricorn, for that which is indicated in Cancer is consummated in Capricorn. Cancer represents the home, the mother. It is personal and emotional, whilst Capricorn represents the group which the unit consciously enters, and also "the father of all that is". The gate of Cancer is entered through the process of transference out of the animal state of consciousness into the human, whilst the gate of Capricorn is entered through initiation. One is inevitable, subconscious and potential; the other is self-initiated, self-conscious and potent. Cancer represents the mass form, the collective animal soul; Capricorn represents the group, the universal soul.

Cancer was originally called the birth month of Jesus. Capricorn is, as we know, the birth month of the Christ, and on the twenty-fifth of December down the centuries the birth of the world saviour has been celebrated; but in very ancient days, the birthday of the infant sun gods was in Cancer. We are told:

"The birthday of the infant Jesus, being arbitrarily set by the priests, produces a serious discrepancy, as we are told he was born in a manger. The manger is found in the sign of the summer solstice, the constellation Cancer, which was called the gate of the sun through which souls were said to descend from their heavenly home to earth, just as at the winter solstice in December, they were said to return to their heavenly or celestial home, the constellation Capricorn, the other gate of the sun. Capricorn was the sign from which sungods were said to be born at the winter solstice and made sacred to the sons of light".

(E. Valentia Straiton, *The Celestial Ship of the North* Vol. II, p.205).

Symbols

The astrological symbol for the sign Cancer has no relation at all to the crab. It is composed of two "asses" tails, and these again link up the gospel story with the story of the manger. In connection with the birth of Jesus two asses appear, the one on which the Virgin rode down to Bethlehem, prior to the birth, and the other on which she rode to Egypt, after the birth. Close to the sign Cancer are two bright stars, one called *Asellus Borealis,* or the northern ass, and the other, *Asellus Australis*, or the southern ass. (There is also the third time, when Christ rode into Jerusalem during his brief moment of triumph on Palm Sunday seated on the back of an ass, a symbol of patience and humility the crown jewels of greatness. So do not decry this symbol.)

Someone has used the following words to express the cadence of Cancer when first entered: "A sorrowful little voice underground, a low, half-captured, half-evasive melody".

Not yet has the work been consummated. All that is to be heard is the note of possible achievement. All that is to be found is a deep inner urge and discontent which gradually becomes so strong that it lifts the hidden, struggling individual out of his environment of stabilised world condition and makes him the earnest aspirant, who knows no rest until he has emerged out of the water and climbed steadily on until he finds himself on the summit of the mount in Capricorn, the birth not the consummation of the world saviour. "Christ was born in Capricorn, fulfilled the law under Saturn, initiated the era of intelligent brotherhood under Venus, and is the perfect example of the Capricorn initiate, who becomes the world server in Aquarius; and the world saviour in Pisces. Cancer admits the soul into the world centre which we call humanity. Capricorn admits the soul into conscious participation in the life of that world centre which we call the Hierarchy".

Esoteric Astrology, p.168

The Three Symbolic Constellations

Jesus is often called the Good Shepherd, and he has been depicted many times as the shepherd leading his sheep. The thought of the sheepfold has been closely associated in the minds of people with Christ. Connected with the sign Cancer are three constellations: Ursa Major, Ursa Minor and Argo. The common occidental names for the two former are the Great Bear and the Little Bear, but it is one of the mysteries of astronomy as to how the name "bear" came to be associated with either of these groups of stars, for in the Chaldean, Persian, Indian and Egyptian zodiacs, no bear is found. The names most commonly used are those of "the sheepfold", or "the flock of sheep", and an analysis of the Hebrew and Arabic names for the stars found in these constellations will be found to prove the fact that the ancient names signify "the lesser flock", "the sheepfold", "the sheep", and "the ship". In the thirty-fourth chapter of Ezekiel and in the tenth chapter of St. John, is much that has reference to these constellations.

Ursa Minor is famous because the brightest star in it is the pole star, the north star. In the symbolism of these two constellations we have held before us the thought of the mass or group, which is the significant influence of the work carried forward in the sign Cancer, and in the symbolism of the north star we have the thought of a lode star, a magnetic attraction, which guides the pilgrim back home. Many esotericists hold the belief that the human family, the fourth kingdom in nature, gradually came into being during the two thousand years, approximately, when our sun was in Cancer.

The thought of a mass of animals, of set boundaries within which these sheep or animals were confined, and the thought of a magnetic centre of attraction, are symbolically portrayed for us also in the Masonic tradition. In Kircher's Egyptian Planisphere, Argo is represented by two galleys (as we have two sheepfolds), whose prows are surmounted by rams' heads, and the stern of one of them ends in a fish's tail. Note, therefore, how we have here held pictorially in front of us the consummation in Capricorn, wherein the goat scales the mountain top. We also have the portrayal of that greater cycle which includes the progress of the soul from Cancer to Capricorn, but which begins in Aries, the ram, and ends in Pisces, the fishes. A close analysis of the symbolism of the zodiacal signs deepens in one the strong conviction of the eternal picturing of truth and the constant holding before our eyes of the story of the evolution of matter in form, of consciousness, of spirit and of life.

Argo stretches all the way from Cancer to Capricorn and is one of the largest of the constellations. It has in it sixty-four stars, of which the brightest is Canopus. Its symbolism, therefore, covers the life of the aspirant from the time he takes incarnation until he has reached his goal. We use the word "ship" quite frequently in a symbolic sense, speaking of the "ship of state", the "ship of salvation", and conveying ever the idea of security, of progress, and of the achieving of a way out, of the making of a journey and of the carrying of a vast crowd of pilgrims in search of golden treasure or a new and freer home.

The pilgrims are equipped with instinct, and as they pass through the various constellations covered by this immense sign, that instinct demonstrates as intellect in a human being as he develops self-consciousness and emerges from out the purely animal stage, until the time comes when, having progressed around and around the zodiac, the aspirant finds himself again in Cancer, faced with the problem of finding that elusive, sensitive, and deeply occult, or hidden, spiritual intuition which will guide him in his now lonely journey; the aspirant is no longer identified and lost in the mass; he is no longer one of the sheep, safely guarded in the sheepfold; he is no longer one of the great herd of emigrants, but he has emerged out of the mass and has started on the lonely way of all disciples. Then he treads the path of tribulation, of test and trial, wrestling by himself as an individual, from Leo to Capricorn, until the time comes when, with the aid of instinct, intellect and intuition, and driven by the urge of the Christ life, he again merges himself with the mass and becomes identified with the group. He then becomes the world server in Aquarius and has no sense of separateness.

The Lesson of the Labour

We have seen that the hind or doe, for which Hercules sought, was sacred to Artemis, the moon, but was also claimed by Diana, the huntress of the heavens, and by Apollo the sun god. One of the things that is often forgotten by students of psychology and those who probe the unfolding consciousness of

man, is the fact that there are no sharp distinctions bet.. __
various aspects of man's nature, but that all are phases of one
reality. The words instinct, intellect and intuition, are but varying aspects of consciousness and of response to environment
and to the world in which the human being finds himself. Man
is an animal, and in company with the animal, he possesses the
quality of instinct and of instinctual response to his environment. Instinct is the consciousness of the form and of the cell
life, the mode of awareness of the form, and, therefore, Artemis,
the moon, who rules over the form, claims the sacred hind. In
its own place, animal instinct is as divine as those other qualities
which we regard as more strictly spiritual.

But man is also a human being; he is rational; he can
analyse, criticise, and he possesses that something which we
call the mind, and that faculty of intellectual perception and response, which differentiates him from the animal, which opens
up to him a new field of awareness, but which is, nevertheless,
simply an extension of his response apparatus and the development of the instinct into intellect. Through the one he becomes
aware of the world of physical contacts and of emotional conditions; through the other he becomes aware of the world of
thought and of ideas, and thus is a human being. When he has
reached that stage of intelligent and instinctual awareness, then
"Eurystheus" indicates to him that there is another world of
which he can become equally aware, but which has its own
method of contact and its own response apparatus.

Diana, the huntress, claimed the doe, because to her the
doe is the intellect and man is the great seeker, the great hunter
before the Lord. But the doe had another and more elusive
form, and for this Hercules, the aspirant, sought. For a life
cycle, we are told, he hunted. It was not the doe, the instinct,
for which he looked; it was not the doe, the intellect, that was
the object of his search. It was something else, and for this he
spent a life cycle hunting. Finally, we read, he captured it and
carried it into the temple, where it was claimed by the sun god

who in the doe recognised the spiritual intuition, that extension of consciousness, that highly developed sense of awareness, which gives to the disciple a vision of new fields of contact and opens up for him a new world of being. We are told that the battle is still going on between Apollo, the sun god, who knew that the doe was the intuition, Diana, huntress of the heavens, who knew it was intellect, and Artemis, the moon, who thought that it was only instinct. Both goddess claimants have a point and the problem of all disciples is to use the instinct correctly, in its right place, and in its proper way. He must learn to use the intellect under the influence of Diana, the huntress, daughter of the sun, and through it become *en rapport* with the world of human ideas and research. He must learn to carry that capacity of his into the temple of the Lord and there to see it transmuted into intuition, and through the intuition become aware of the things of spirit and of those spiritual realities which neither instinct nor intellect can reveal to him. (And again and again the sons of men, who are also sons of God, must recapture these spiritual realities, upon the endless Way.)

LABOUR V.

THE SLAYING OF THE NEMEAN LION
(Leo, July 22nd-August 21st)

The Myth

The great Presiding One sat within the Council Chamber of the Lord and there discussed the plan of God for all the sons of men, who are the sons of God. The Teacher stood at his right hand and listened to his words. And Hercules rested from his labours.

And the great Presiding One, within the Council Chamber of the Lord, watched the tired warrior rest and watched his thoughts. He said then to the Teacher who stood close to his hand within the Council Chamber of the Lord: "The time for a dread labour now draws near. This man, who is a son of man and yet a son of God, must be prepared. Let him look well unto the weapons that he owns and let him burnish bright his shield, and dip his arrows in a lethal brew, for dire and dread is the labour just ahead. Let him prepare."

But Hercules, resting from his labours, wot not the trial which lay just ahead. He felt his courage strong. He rested from his labours, and time and time again, past the fourth Gate he chased the sacred doe clear to the temple of the Lord. Time came wherein the timid hind knew well the hunter who pursued her, and gently came at his command. Thus time and time again, he placed the doe upon his heart and sought the temple of the Lord. Thus rested he.

Before the fifth great Gate stood Hercules, armed to the teeth with all the gifts of war and warriors, and as he stood the watching gods marked his firm step, his eager eye, his ready hand. But deep within his heart was questioning.

"What do I here?" he said. "What is the test and wherefore do I seek to pass this Gate?" and speaking thus he waited, listening for a voice. "What do I here, O Teacher of my life, armed, as you see, with the full panoply of war? What do I here?"

"A call has sounded forth, O Hercules, a call of deep distress. Your outer ears have not responded to that call, and yet the inner ear knows well the need, for it hath heard a voice, aye, many voices, telling you of need and urging you to venture forth. The people of Nemea seek your aid. They are in deep distress. Word of your prowess has gone forth. They seek that you should kill the lion that devastates their land, taking its toll of men".

"Is that the savage sound I hear?" asked Hercules. "Is it the roaring of a lion I hear, upon the evening air?" The Teacher said: "Go, seek the lion which ravages the land lying upon the further side of the fifth Gate. The people of this ravaged land live silently behind locked doors. Forth to their tasks they venture not, nor till their land, nor sow. From north to south, from east to west the lion prowls and prowling seizes all who cross his path. His shocking roar is heard throughout the night and all are trembling behind locked doors. What will you do, O Hercules? What will you do?"

And Hercules, with listening ear, responded to the need. Upon the nearer side of the great Gate which guarded firm the country of Nemea, he dropped the panoply of war, retaining for his use the club, cut by his hands from a young and springing tree. "What do you now, O son of man, who are likewise a son of God? Where are your arms and where your strong defence?" "This fine array of arms but loads me down, retards my speed and hinders my departure on the Way. I shall require naught but my stalwart club, and with this club and my stout heart, I go upon my way to seek the lion. Send word unto the people of Nemea that I go upon the Way, and bid them cast out fear".

* * *

From place to place passed Hercules, seeking the lion. He found the people of Nemea, hiding behind locked doors, save but a few who ventured forth because of need or desperation. They trod the highway in the light of day, yet full of fear. They greeted Hercules with joy at first, with questioning later, as they saw the manner of his travel; no arms, small knowledge of the ways of lions, and naught save a frail wooden club. "Where are your arms, O Hercules? Have you not fear? Why seek the lion without defence? Go find your weapons and your shield. The lion is fierce and strong, and numbers vast he has devoured. Why take this chance? Go seek your arms and panoply of strength". But silently, without response, the son of man, who was the son of God, went forth upon the Way, seeking the footstep of the lion and following its voice"

"The lion is where?" asked Hercules. "The lion is here", came the reply. "No, there", enjoined a voice of fear. "Not so", replied a third, "I heard its roar about the mountain wild this week". "And I, likewise, within this valley where we stand". And yet another said: "I saw its tracks upon a path I trod, so, Hercules, list to my voice and track him to his lair".

* * *

Thus Hercules pursued his way, afraid yet unafraid; alone, yet not alone, for on the trail he followed others stood, and followed him with hope and fearful tremblings. For days and several nights he searched the Way and listened for the lion's roar whilst the people of Nemea crouched down behind closed doors.

Suddenly he saw the lion. Upon the edge of a deep thicket of young trees it stood. Seeing an enemy draw near and one who seemed quite unafraid, the lion roared, and with his roar the young trees shook, the Nemeans fled and Hercules stood still.

Hercules grasped his bow and sheath of arrows and with sure hand and eye of skill planted an arrow in the shoulder of the lion. Straight to the mark it flew. Upon the ground the arrow fell and failed to pierce the shoulder of the lion. Again and yet again, he shot the lion until there rested not an arrow in his quiver. Then towards him came the lion, untouched, unscathed and fierce with rage, quite unafraid. Throwing his bow upon the ground, the son of man, who is a son of God, rushed with wild shouting towards the lion who stood upon the Way, blocking his path, amazed at prowess hitherto unmet. For Hercules came on. Suddenly the lion turned and rushed ahead of Hercules into a thicket on the rocky sides of the sharp mountain way.

And so the two went on. And suddenly, as he travelled on the Way, the lion disappeared and was no more seen or heard.

Hercules paused upon the Way and silent stood. He searched on every hand, grasping his trusty club, the weapon he himself had made, the gift that to himself he had bequeathed in days long past, his trusty club. On every hand he sought; on every way he passed, travelling from point to point upon the narrow way that ran athwart the mountain side. Suddenly, upon a cave he came and from the cave there came a lusty roar, a rumbling savage voice which seemed to bid him stay or lose his life. And Hercules stood still, shouting unto the people of the land: "The lion is here. Await the deed that I shall do". And Hercules, who is a son of man and yet a son of God, entered that cave and passed throughout its darkened length into the light of day and found no lion, only another opening in the cave that led into the light of day. And as he stood, he heard the lion behind him, not before"

"What shall I do?" said Hercules unto himself, "this cave has openings twain and as I enter one the lion passes out and enters by the one I left behind. What shall I do? Weapons avail me not. How kill this lion and save the people from its teeth? What shall I do?"

And as he cast about for things to do and listened to the roaring of the lion, he saw some piles of wood and sticks lying in great profusion near his hand. Pulling them towards him, dragging with his might, he placed the piles of sticks and bundles of small twigs within the opening near at hand and piled them there, blocking the way into the light of day, both in and out, and shutting both himself and the fierce lion within the cave. Then turned and faced the lion.

With his two hands he grasped the lion, holding it close and choking it. Near was its breath and blasting in his face. Yet still he held its throat and choked the lion. Feebler and feebler grew the roars of hate and fear; weaker and weaker grew the enemy of man; lower and lower sank the lion, yet Hercules held on. And thus he killed the lion with his two hands, without his arms and through his own great strength.

He killed the lion and stripped its skin, shewing it to the people, without the entrance of the cave. "The lion is dead",they cried, "the lion is dead. We now can live and till our lands and sow the needed seeds and walk in peace together. The lion is dead and great is our deliverer, the son of man, who is a son of God, named Hercules."

* * *

Thus Hercules returned in triumph to the One Who sent him forth to test his strength, to serve and meet the need of those in dire distress. He laid the lion's skin beneath the feet of him who was the Teacher of his life, and gained permission to wear the skin in place of that already worn and used.

"The deed is done. The people now stand free. There is no fear. The lion is dead. With my own hands I strangled thus the lion and slaughtered it."

"Again, O Hercules, you slew a lion. Again you strangled him. The lion and serpents must be slain again and once again. Well done, my son, go rest in peace with those you have released from fear. Labour the fifth is over and I go to tell the great Presiding One, who sitteth waiting in the Council Chamber of the Lord. Rest thou in peace".

And from the Council Chamber came the voice: I KNOW THE TIBETAN.

The Number Five

In the fifth sign, Leo, Hercules performs that one of his labours which is the best known historically, for the slaying of the Nemean lion has always been associated with Hercules, though it is interesting to note that this famous labour has no relation to the lion's skin which Hercules always wore. That was the skin of the lion that he slew before he undertook his labours and which was his first act of service. Through that act he demonstrated that he was ready for testing and training.

This is one of the most interesting labours numerically, and in order to understand it thoroughly and grasp its true significance, we must take account of the number five which distinguishes it. From the standpoint of the esotericist, five is the number of man, because man is a divine son of God, plus the quaternary which consists of the lower fourfold nature, the mental body, emotional body, vital body and physical sheath. In the language of the psychologists, man is a self, a continuation of mental and emotional states, vitality, and the response apparatus of the physical body. These four we have seen brought into relation to the involving soul, in the four preceding signs.

In Aries, the soul took to itself that type of matter which would enable it to be in relation to the world of ideas. It clothed itself in a mental sheath. It added to individuality those combinations of mental substance through which it could best express itself. And man became a thinking soul. In Taurus, the desire world was contacted and a similar procedure pursued. The means of sentiently contacting the world of feeling and emotion were developed and man became a sentient soul. In Gemini, a new and vital energy body was constructed by the bringing together of the energies of soul and matter, and man became a living soul, for the two poles were en rapport, and the vital or etheric body came into being. In Cancer, which is the sign of physical birth and of the identification of the unit with the mass, the work of incarnation was completed and the four-fold nature was manifested. Man became a living actor on the physical plane. But it is in Leo that man becomes what is oc-cultly called the five-pointed star, for that star stands as the sym-bol of individualisation, of humanity, of the human being who knows himself to be an individual and becomes aware of him-self as the Self. It is in this sign that we begin to use the words, "I", and "my", and "mine".

The Ageless Wisdom of the east tells us that the number five is the most occult and the most deeply significant of the numbers. It claims that the group of celestial and spiritual be-ings, who took incarnation on earth, manifested through the quaternary, and thus brought into existence the human family, were the fifth group of divine lives and that they combined within themselves, therefore, the dual attributes of the uni-verse, the spiritual and physical, They unified in themselves the two poles. They were exoteric and esoteric; they were ob-jective and subjective. Thus we have the number ten, which is regarded as the number of human perfection and of com-pletion, the number of a perfectly developed and unfolded human being, and of the balance achieved between spirit and matter. But it is the number wherein spirit does *not* dominate matter; it is the number of the aspirant whose objective it is to subordinate matter to the uses of spirit and, therefore, upset the balance of the number ten.

The ancient scriptures of the east use some interesting phrases to express the nature of these celestial beings who are the men of our time, who are ourselves, who are the sons of God in incarnation. They are called Lords of Knowledge and of Wis-dom, Lords of Will and of Sacrifice, Lords of Boundless Devo-tion, and these terms, characterising the spiritual entity dwelling in every human form, merit the closest consideration of those who seek to tread the round of the zodiac as conscious individuals with a spiritual goal. Through our own will and in full knowledge we are here. In order to raise matter into heaven, we have come into manifested existence. In essence and in reality, man is not what he appears to be. He is essentially what he will demonstrate in Aquarius, the opposite sign to Leo. He will then be the man with a universal consciousness, in contradistinction to the self-assertive individuality of the Leo type. The individual in Leo becomes the initiate in Capricorn, and demonstrates as the complete man in Aquarius, and this has only been possible because of the boundless devotion to a dimly sensed objective that has carried him round and round the zodiac until full self-consciousness has been achieved.

The appropriateness and the relation of the fifth Commandment to the fifth labour and the fifth sign thus becomes apparent. "Honour thy father and thy mother; that thy days may be long in the land which the Lord thy God giveth thee", for in Leo, Father-spirit and Mother-matter meet in the individual and their union produces that conscious entity which we call the soul or the Self. Just, however; as this is the sign wherein man recognises himself as the individual and begins the cycle of experience wherein he acquires knowledge, so it is the sign wherein the self-conscious man begins his training for initiation. It is in this sign that we have the last of the tests on the probationary path. When the labour of this sign ends, definite training for initiation in Capricorn is begun. Some measure of control of thought has been gained in Aries, and some power to transmute desire has been achieved in Taurus. The apples of wisdom have been gathered in Gemini and the distinction between wisdom and knowledge has been somewhat learned, whilst the necessity of transmuting instinct and intellect into intuition and the carrying of them both into the Temple of the Lord has been grasped in Cancer.

The Story of the Myth

After a relatively simple labour in Cancer and one that was quite free from danger and peril, Eurystheus imposes upon Hercules the tremendous task of slaying the Nemean lion, which was devastating the countryside. For a long period the lion had been a destructive force and people were unable to do anything about it. Hercules found that the only way in which he could achieve his object was to chase the lion in ever-narrowing circles until he had cornered it in a cave. This he proceeded to do and eventually tracked it to its lair.

Having succeeded in this preliminary stage, he then made the unpleasant discovery that the cave had two openings and that as fast as he chased the lion in at one it emerged at the other. There was nothing for it, therefore, but to stop the chase and to block one of the openings to the cave, and this Hercules did. Then he chased the lion into the cave through the unblocked opening and, leaving all weapons behind, even the club which he had himself made, he entered the cave and with his two hands choked the lion to death. That was an encounter that took place unseen by anybody; Hercules and the lion in the dark and the gloom of the cave taking part, both of them, in a struggle which had to be to the death.

The Field of the Labour

The sign Leo is one of the four arms of the fixed cross in the heavens, the cross on which the Cosmic Christ and the individual Christ are ever crucified. Perhaps the word "crucified" would have a true significance if we substituted for it the word "sacrificed", for in the unfoldment of the Christ consciousness in the form, stage by stage, various aspects of the divine nature are seen as being sacrificed.

In Taurus, the symbol of creative force expressing itself through desire, we see the lower aspect of the divine creative force, sexual desire, transmuted into, or sacrificed to, its higher aspect. It had to be raised up into heaven.

In Leo, we see cosmic mind working out in the individual as the lower reasoning mind, and this lower aspect has likewise to be sacrificed and the little mind of man must be subordinated to the universal mind. In Scorpio, which is the third arm of the fixed cross, we find cosmic love or cosmic attraction. There it is shown in its lower aspect, and this we call the great Illusion; and in Scorpio we see the aspirant upon the cross, sacrificing illusion to reality. In Aquarius, we have the light of the universal consciousness irradiating the human being and bringing about the sacrifice of the individual life and its merging in the universal whole. This is the true crucifixion: the sacrifice of the reflection to the reality, of the lower aspect to the higher and of the individual unit to the great sum total. It was these characteristics that the Christ so marvellously demonstrated. He showed himself as the Creator. He showed himself as functioning under the influence of the illuminated mind; he personified in himself the love of God, and he announced himself as the Light of the World. The problem before Hercules, therefore, was the problem of the sign; the crucifixion of the lower self and the conquering of individual self-assertion.

Originally the zodiac consisted only of ten constellations and, at some date practically unknown, the two constellations, Leo and Virgo, were one symbol. Perhaps the mystery of the sphinx is connected with this, for in the sphinx we have the lion with a woman's head, Leo with Virgo, the symbol of the lion or kingly soul, and its relation to the matter or Mother aspect. It may, therefore, signify the two polarities, masculine and feminine, positive and negative.

In this constellation is the exceedingly bright star, which is one of the four royal stars of the heavens. It is called *Regulus,* the Ruler, the Lawgiver, holding in its significance the thought that man can now be a law unto himself, for he has that within him which is the king or the ruler. Hidden in the constellation is also a vivid group of stars, called "the sickle". To the ancient initiates, who saw all the external constellations as personifications of forces and as symbols of an unfolding drama vaster than even they could understand, the constellation conveyed three major thoughts: first, that man was the ruler, the king, God incarnate, an individual son of God; second, the man was governed by law, the law of nature, the law that he makes for himself, and the spiritual law to which he will eventually subordinate himself; third, that the work of an individual is to apply the sickle and to cut out, or cut down, that which hinders the application of the spiritual law and so hinders the flowering forth of the soul.

The constellation Leo has in it ninety-five stars, two of them of the first magnitude. Its Egyptian name, we are told, meant "a pouring out", the Nile giving its fullest irrigation at that season. This has also an interesting esoteric significance for, according to the teaching of the Ageless Wisdom, the human family came into existence through what is technically called "the third outpouring", which was the term given to the coming-in of a great tide of souls into the animal bodies and, therefore, the formation of the human family composed of individual units. Another technical term for this third outpouring is "individualisation", becoming an individual with self-awareness, thus linking it up with the great happenings in the sign, Leo.

The ninety-five stars in this constellation also have numerical significance for we have there 9 x 10 + 5. Nine is the number of initiation, ten is the number of human perfection, five is the number of man, and thus in this grouping of stars we have the story of man, of the personality, the initiate and his ultimate spiritual achievement.

The Three Symbolic Constellations

There is an immense constellation called *Hydra,* the serpent, associated with the sign Leo. We find also *Crater,* the cup, and *Corvus,* the raven. All three sum up in their significance the problem of the man who is seeking initiation. They picture to him distinctly and clearly the work that he has to do. As Leo, the king, the soul, starts upon his work, he realises that he has the cup of suffering and of experience to drink, the serpent of illusion to overcome, and the bird of prey to eliminate *Hydra*, the serpent, in the ancient pictures is portrayed as a female serpent. It covers more than a hundred degrees and lies beneath the three constellations, Cancer, Leo and Virgo.

In Scorpio, this serpent of matter or of illusion, with which the soul has identified itself for so long, is finally overcome. It has in it sixty stars, and again we come in touch with a significant number, for six is the number of mind, of the creative work of the universal Mind, and of the six days of creation. In the sixth sign, Virgo, we have the completed form. We are told in the Book of Revelations that the mark of the Beast is 666, and *Hydra,* the serpent, lies under three constellations and its number 6 is, therefore, three times potent. Ten is the number of completion. Six expresses, therefore, the limitations of the body nature working through form and the utilisation of the personality; it symbolises God in nature, whether cosmically or individually. *Hydra*, the serpent, represents the matter aspect, as it veils and hides the soul.

The *Crater,* or the cup, has in it thirteen stars of ordinary magnitude and about ninety small stars, though some books of astronomy say three brilliant stars and ninety small. So we have again the number of matter, or of form-taking, and the number of what is called "apostasy", and of "the turning of the back", as Judas Iscariot did, upon the soul or Christ aspect. This cup forms really part of the body of the *Hydra,* for the stars at the foot of the cup form part of the body of the *Serpent* and both constellations claim them. It is the cup that every human being has to drink, full of that which he has distilled out of his experience in matter. It is the cup of obligation in certain of the ancient Masonic rituals, and symbolizes the drinking of that which we have ourselves brewed. In other words, the same truth can be expressed in the words of the Christian Bible, "As a man soweth, so shall he also reap".

Then we have, thirdly, *Corvus;* the raven, that stands upon *Hydra,* the serpent, and pecks at it. It has nine stars, again the number of initiation. The Old Testament started with a raven, the New Testament starts with a dove. Experience starts with the bird of matter and ends with the bird of spirit. It is interesting to note that in Aquarius, the consummating sign to Leo, we find *Cygnus,* the swan, the symbol of the bird of spirit. In *The Voice of the Silence* we read: "And then thou canst repose between the wings of the great bird. Aye, sweet to rest between the wings of that which is not born, nor dies, but is the Aum throughout eternal ages". And in a footnote H.P.B., referring to the bird or swan, quotes: "Says the *Rig- Veda* . . . The syllable *A* is considered to be the bird Hamsa's right wing, *U* its left, and *M* its tail.."
                                    (*The Chakras* by C. W. Leadbeater)

In the zodiac of Denderah, Leo and the three attendant constellations are pictured as forming one great sign, for the lion is seen treading on the serpent. *Corvus,* the raven, is perched upon the lion's shoulder, while below is a plumed female figure (again, the symbol of matter) holding out two cups, for there is ever the cup which symbolises the cup of experience, the cup of penalty. The cup is the cup which is offered to the initiate, to which Christ referred in the Garden of Gethsemane, when he pleaded that the cup be taken away from him, but which he ended by drinking.

So Hercules, the aspirant, expressing himself in Leo, visions the great battle that lies ahead of him, knows that his past must work out to fulfilment in the future, knows that before he can climb the mountain in Capricorn he must slay the *Hydra,* and knows that he must no longer be the raven, but must manifest as *Aquila*, the eagle of Scorpio, and as *Cygnus,* the swan, in Aquarius. This he must begin to do in Leo, by demonstrating the power to dare, by facing the terrific struggle that lies ahead of him in the next three signs and by the slaying of the lion of his own nature (king of beasts) alone and unaided, and so earn the power to overcome the *Hydra*, in Scorpio.

The Lesson of the Labour

Two thoughts, taken out of the Christian Bible, summarise the lesson of this labour. In St. Peter's *Epistle* we find these words: "Your adversary, the devil, like a roaring lion walketh about, seeking whom he may devour", and in *Revelations* 5:5, we find the words, "Behold, the Lion of the tribe of Judah the Root of David, hath prevailed to open the book, and to loose the seven seals thereof".

Hercules, the aspirant, the soul, symbolised the lion, the prince, the king, the ruler, and because of this he symbolically wore the lion's skin. The Nemean lion stands essentially for the co-ordinated, dominant personality, for the aspirant has always to be a highly evolved individual.

With the triple aspects of the lower personal self fused and blended and, therefore, potent beyond the average, the aspirant often becomes a somewhat trying and difficult person. He has a mind and he is using it. His emotions are controlled, or else are so blended with his mental reactions that they are unusually powerful; hence, he is exceedingly individual, often very aggressive, self-confident and self-satisfied, and his personality is, therefore, a devastating force in the family group, society, or organisation with which he may be affiliated. Therefore, the aspirant, the lion of Judah, has to slay the lion of his personality. Having emerged out of the mass, and developed individuality, he then has to slay that which he has created; he has to render helpless that which has been the great protecting agent up to the present time. Selfishness, the self-protecting instinct, has to give place to unselfishness, which is literally the subordination of the self to the whole.

Therefore, the Nemean lion symbolises the powerful personality running wild and menacing the peace of the countryside. What is the lesson intended to be learned by the fact that Hercules tracked the lion to a cave that had two openings? Why did he stop up one opening and enter in through the other? And what is the spiritual teaching underlying the tradition that he there slew the lion with his bare hands?

Many of these old stories have held the true significance of their meaning unfathomed for thousands of years, and it is only in this day and generation that the true esoteric meaning can possibly emerge. The interesting fact about the period in which we now live is that it marks a unique development in racial unfoldment. There have always been manifestations of the sun gods, and this labour of Hercules has again and again been enacted by a few here and a few there. Every nation has produced highly evolved aspirants who track the lion of the personality down into the cave and there master it. But, relatively, in relation to the myriads of human units, they have constituted a very small minority. Now we have a world full of aspirants; the coming generation in all nations will produce its thousands of disciples and already tens of thousands are seeking the Way. People are now very individual, the world is full of *personalities*, and the time has come when the lion of the tribe of Judah must prevail over the lion of the personal self. We are not alone in our struggle, as Hercules was, but we form part of a great group of sun gods, who are struggling with the tests preparatory to initiation, and with the problems that will draw out the full powers of the soul.

In Capricorn we shall climb the mountaintop, and entering now, as we are, the Aquarian cycle, the aspirants of the race are in a position to begin to learn the lesson of service and universal consciousness. When, in two thousand years' time, we begin to enter Capricorn, there will then be a tremendous gathering-in of initiates, and the scaling of the mount of initiation and the mount of transfiguration by many hundreds of disciples. In the meantime, the lion of the personality has to be dealt with and the cave entered.

In the symbolism of the scriptures of the world, the most momentous happenings are enacted in one of two places: in the cave or on the mountain. The Christ is born in the cave; the personality is overcome in the cave; the voice of the Lord is heard in the cave, the Christ consciousness is nurtured in the cave of the heart, but after the cave experiences the mountain of transfiguration is climbed, the mount of crucifixion is achieved, to be succeeded finally by the mountain of ascension.

I would like here to give the technical, perhaps more scientific, interpretation of this cave which Hercules entered. The Aryan race, to which we belong, is one of keen mental development, and the consciousness of people everywhere is shifting steadily out of the emotional nature, and so out of the solar plexus centre, into the mental body and, therefore, into the head. There is in the head a little cave, a small bony structure which shields and guards one of the most important glands in the body, the pituitary. When this gland is in full and proper functioning activity, we shall have a personality rounded-out and active, self-controlled, with pronounced mental activity and endurance.

This pituitary body is dual in its configuration: in one of its lobes, the frontal or ante-pituitary, is to be found the seat of the reasoning mind, intellectuality, and in the other, the post-pituitary, is the seat of the emotional, imaginative nature. It is also said that this gland co-ordinates the others, controls growth and is essential to life. It is interesting that Berman defines intellectuality as the "capacity of the mind to control its environment by concepts and abstract ideas". Where there is a lack of development of this gland you may find both emotional and mental deficiency. Many endocrinologists and psychologists have expressed themselves along similar lines.* It is in this cave that the lion of the developed personality or individuality has its lair and it is here that the sun god, Hercules, must conquer.

---

*The Soul and Its Mechanism by Alice A. Bailey. Lucis Publishing Company, New York, N.Y, and the Lucis Press Limited, London.

For centuries the Egyptians, and especially the Hindus, have known of the chakras or force-centres in the etheric body. The discovery of the endocrine system shows corresponding physical glands in the same locations. One of these, the pituitary body, with its two lobes, symbolises the cave with two openings, one of which Hercules had to close before he could control the personality by the higher mind. For it was only when he had blocked the opening of the personal emotions (post-pituitary), thrown away even his trusty club, refused symbolically to lead any longer a personal, selfish life, that he could, entering by the opening represented by the ante-pituitary, subdue the lion of the personality in the cave. These correlations are so exact that they present in little and in large an awesome testimony to the unflawed integrity of the Plan. "As above so below". A striking correlation between biological and spiritual truths.

LABOUR VI.

SEIZING THE GIRDLE OF HIPPOLYTE*
(Virgo, August 22nd-September 21st)

The Myth

The great Presiding One called unto him the Teacher watching over Hercules. "The time is drawing near", he said, "how fares the son of man who is a son of God? Is he prepared again to venture forth and try his mettle with a foe of a different sort? Can he now pass the sixth great Gate?"

And the Teacher answered: "Yes". He was assured within himself that when the word went forth the disciple would arise to labours new, and this he told the great Presiding One within the Council Chamber of the Lord.

And then the word went forth. "Arise, O Hercules, and pass the sixth great Gate". Another word likewise went forth, though not to Hercules, but unto those who dwelt upon the shores of the great sea. They listened and they heard.

Upon those shores dwelt the great queen, who reigned o'er all the women of the then known world. They were her vassals and her warriors bold. Within her realm, of men not one was found. Only the women, gathered round their queen. Within the temple of the moon they daily worshipped and there they sacrificed to Mars, the god of war.

---

*From now on the chapters will be based on the informal lectures given by A.A.B., her finished material for a proposed book having run out. Therefore, a rewrite will be offered plus material from *Esoteric Astrology* and from *The Gifts of the Spirit* by Dane Rudhyar, neither of which had appeared at the time the lectures were given in 1937.

Back from their annual visit to the haunts of men they came. Within the temple precincts they awaited word from Hippolyte, their queen, who stood upon the steps of the high altar, wearing the girdle given her by Venus, queen of love. This girdle was a symbol, a symbol of unity achieved through struggle, conflict, strife, a symbol of motherhood and of the sacred Child to whom all human life is truly turned.

"Word has gone forth", said she, "that on his way there comes a warrior whose name is Hercules, a son of man and yet a son of God; to him I must give up this girdle which I wear. Shall we obey the word, O Amazons, or shall we fight the word of God?" And as they listened to her words and as they pondered o'er the problem, again a word went forth, saying that he was there, ahead of time, waiting without to seize the sacred girdle of the fighting queen.

Forth to the son of God who was likewise a son of man went Hippolyte, the warrior queen. He fought and struggled with her and listened not to the fair words she strove to speak. He wrenched the girdle from her, only to find her hands held out and offering him the gift, offering the symbol of unity and love, of sacrifice and faith. Yet, grasping it, he slaughtered her, killing the one who dowered him with that which he required. And as he stood beside the dying queen, aghast at that which he had done, he heard his Teacher speak:

"My son, why slay that which is needed, close and dear? Why kill the one you love, the giver of good gifts, custodian of the possible? Why kill the mother of the sacred Child? Again, we mark a failure. Again you have not understood. Redeem this moment, e'er again you seek my face".

Silence fell and Hercules, gathering the girdle to his breast, sought out the homeward way, leaving the women sorrowing, bereft of leadership and love.

* * *

Unto the shores of the great sea again came Hercules. Close to the rocky shore he saw a monster of the deep, holding between his jaws poor Hesione. Her shrieks and sighs rose to high heaven and smote the ears of Hercules, lost in regret and knowing not the path he trod. Unto her help he promptly rushed, but rushed too late. She disappeared within the cavernous throat of the sea serpent, that monster of ill fame. But losing sight of self, this son of man who was a son of God breasted the waves and reached the monster, who, turning towards the man with swift attack and roaring loud, opened his mouth. Down the red tunnel of his throat rushed Hercules, in search of Hesione; finding her deep within the belly of the monster. With his left arm he seized her, and held her close whilst with his trusty sword he hewed his way from out the belly of the serpent into the light of day. And so he rescued her, balancing thus his previous deed of death. For such is life: an act of death, a deed of life, and thus the sons of men, who are the sons of God, learn wisdom, balance and the way to walk with God.

From out the Council Chamber of the Lord, the great Presiding One looked on. And from his post beside, the Teacher too looked on. Through the sixth Gate again passed Hercules, and seeing this and seeing both the girdle and the maid, the Teacher spoke and said: "Labour the sixth is over. You slaughtered that which cherished you and all unknown and all unrecognised gave unto you the needed love and power. You rescued that which needed you, and thus again the two are one. Ponder anew upon the ways of life, reflecting on the ways of death. Go rest, my son".

THE TIBETAN.

LABOUR VI

Introduction

It is said that, from some aspects, Virgo is the oldest of the zo-diacal signs. Down through the ages, be it Lilith or Isis, Eve or the Virgin Mary, all portray the mother of the world, but it is Mary who at length bears the Child in her arms. And it is in this sign that the Christ consciousness is conceived and nurtured through the period of gestation until at last in Pisces, the opposite sign, the world saviour is born.

As in Leo, this is a cave experience, "in the womb of time", and should be characterised by warmth, quietness, deep experiences and "slow, yet powerful crises". It is a synthetic sign. On this point the Tibetan says: "The symbology of Virgo concerns the whole goal of the evolutionary process, which is to shield, nurture and finally reveal the hidden spiritual reality. This, every form veils but the human form is equipped and fitted to manifest it in a manner different from any other expression of divinity and so make tangible and objective that for which the whole creative process was intended".

Esoteric Astrology, pp. 251-2

This synthetic quality is further emphasised by the fact that eight other signs (all except Leo, Libra and Capricorn) through their planetary rulers pour their energies through Virgo, and the Tibetan calls attention to the fact that we are now entering the eighth sign from Virgo, in other words, the next sign before that in which the Child is brought to birth, the sign which will see many take initiation. It is to be remembered that all men and women pass through all signs, and for those born in Virgo, or having that sign on the ascendant (the eastern point of the chart, indicating the soul purpose of the disciple) these qualities or energies are displayed in many ways, for organisations, arts, sciences, all call for long periods of mental gestation and the struggle of bringing forth new ideas into manifestation.

Another unique feature of Virgo is that it has a triple symbol, which only one other sign, Scorpio, has. This is significant, implying that these two signs are "connected with the growth of Christ consciousness. They mark critical points in the soul's experience, points of integration, wherein the soul is consciously at-one-ing itself with the form and at the same time with spirit". (*Esoteric Astrology,* p. 481). This statement underlies the spiritual theory of Triangles, which are many, and the Tibetan adds these august and arresting words: "Under the will of Deity and the unalterable energy at the heart of the manifested zodiac, they produce the changes in consciousness that make man divine at the close of the world cycle". And further: "It is through the fusing and blending of the three planetary energies, *by the agency of human thought, reacting to zodiacal energies,* that our earth will be transformed into a sacred planet". (*Editor's italics.*) Surely these words expand our vision, deepen our understanding, give us faith in the future of humanity, and strength to co-operate patiently with the present.

Interpretations of the Myth

The story of the myth related that the great Presiding One recognised that this labour was indeed with an enemy "of a different sort". It is interesting that the two labours which Hercules, though he won eventually, performed badly were with his polar opposites, females. In Aries the conquering of the man-eating mares so inflated his ego that he stalked on ahead in pride and left the mares to Abderis, his personality, with the result that they escaped and the labour had to be repeated. "But Abderis lay dead". And in the labour in Virgo, he slayed the queen of the Amazons, though she offered him the girdle, and then he had to rescue another maiden, Hesione, from the belly of the whale, to compensate for the life he had unnecessarily taken.

So the war between the sexes is of ancient origin; indeed is inherent in the duality of humanity and the solar system. To this fact our divorce courts bear loud testimony; and competition arises in business as well as in the home. There are small but important points in the story not to be overlooked. What did Hippolyte contribute to the error? Perhaps this: she proffered to Hercules the girdle of unity, given her by Venus, because she had been told that the Presiding One had so ordered, not because she felt unity. Did she do it under compulsion but with no love? And so she died. Even so we are told that evil must come, but woe betide those by whom it comes, and so Hercules failed to understand his spiritual mission, though he obtained its objective.

Again, one wonders why the Amazons made a yearly sortie into the world of men? Was it to make war on them, or was it to seek unity, in which there was no heart? Was it to seek new members for their man-less world? But God, we are told, looks at the heart. It will come as a shock to many of strict, legally moral views to reflect that an avowed prostitute may be superior to a woman who adds blasphemy to prostitution, when she takes vows in church without love and with no intent to serve, but only to obtain money, security or position. One seldom hears a sermon on the woman taken in adultery, of whom the Christ said, "Neither do I condemn thee. Go in peace and sin no more". All of this seems subtly involved in the myth of the labour in Virgo. Its practical application as well as its cosmic and spiritual significances are startling. We are told that the "*war with purpose* between the sexes is now at a climax".

This time the Teacher did not say merely that the work was badly done. He said without equivocation, "Why kill the mother of the sacred Child? Again we mark a failure. Again you have not understood. Redeem this moment e'er again you seek my face". These were stern words and we should listen to the keynote. "Again you have not understood". And silence fell, and Hercules, gathering the girdle to his breast, sought out the homeward way, leaving the women sorrowing and bereft of leadership and love.

The act of death; then a deed of love when, at the risk of his own life, Hercules rescued Hesione and earned from the

Teacher the words: "Ponder anew upon the ways of life, reflecting on the ways of death. Go rest, my son". We offer no apologies for repeating the words of the myth as told by the Tibetan; they are superlatively beautiful and their mantric power seems destroyed by paraphrasing them.

It is to be noted also that the labour was not described to Hercules as in other cases. The word went out only to the country where the queen of the Amazons ruled her woman's world, all men excluded. It was left for Hercules to understand the nature of the labour, and he did not. Also the Amazons worshipped the moon (the form), and Mars, the god of war; they too did not understand their true function, for Mary is pictured with the moon under her feet, and in her arms the one to be known as the Prince of Peace.

The Two Ways

As always there is a choice for good or evil before the native of a sign, depending on his status of evolution and the degree of sensitivity. Virgo is called the goddess of virtue or of vice. But what is the root meaning of "vice"? "To render ineffective", and that for Virgo is to negate the whole purpose of the sign, for it is said that "the Christ is to her the purpose of existence". The root of "virtue" is the Latin word *vir* meaning "strength", "man", as in "virility". The deep meaning of vice as an ineffectiveness of the spiritual life, reminds one again of the explanation of the saying in one of the Rules of the Road: "For each must know the villainy of each and still love on". For it appears that a villain in this sense is merely a narrow-minded, rather uncouth fellow, a dweller in a small village, who knows nothing beyond his own small ring-pass-not.

How obvious, and what breeders of true tolerance, are these root meanings. Too long have we belaboured the body, the physical, as the root of all evil, when it is really our narrow minds, our hard, small hearts, that cause wrong attitudes and habits; the body being but an automatic response apparatus,

subject to the control of the inner man. Another idea presents
itself in this connection, i.e., that "sin" means literally "anything
that is done amiss". Just not hitting the "bull's eye", the "eye of
illumination" spoken of in Taurus, is a sin for the son of man
who is also a son of God. How perfectly these fundamental
ideas interplay and confirm each other, when we abandon the
complexities of the lower mind. Virgo is also called the "goddess of the two ways", because as the Holy Mother principle
she symbolises matter and also is the custodian of the Christ
life.

It is meaningful that this sixth sign, the number of physical
plane activity, is called the number of the Beast. This idea
seems to have a horrible fascination for many, but what it really
means is that Virgo is a symbol of the triplicity, 6 on the physical plane, 6 on the emotional plane, 6 on the mental plane, not
666 at all.

It is to be remembered that the lion is the king of beasts.
The native attains finally in that sign the rounded-out personality. But in Virgo, the first of the steps towards spirituality is
taken, the soul is called the son of mind, and Virgo is ruled by
Mercury, carrying the energy of the mind.

In this Virgo lecture A.A.B. gave a most interesting sequence of prophetic references to the Virgin as follows:

"Behold, I will bring forth my servant, the *branch*".
(*Zechariah 3:8*). One symbol of Virgo is the woman with the
ear of corn, or the sheaf of wheat, or the branch of fruit in her
arms. Remember also the prophecy in *Isaiah* upon which our
New Testament is based: "And a virgin shall conceive and bring
forth a son", and link up with that verse in *Ephesians* when St.
Paul said that some day we shall attain unto the measure of the
stature of the fullness of Christ. I would remind you that Christ
laid the emphasis again and again on the new birth rather than
on blood sacrifice. The esoteric meaning is "the blood is the
life". We are always too literal. Even as the old practice of offering slain animals at the altar passed, so should pass the idea

of atonement by the blood of Christ. That was born of the medieval guilt complex and the torturing of the physical instrument as a means to produce the dominance of the spirit; when the truth is that the body should be attuned to the soul and bring its beauty into manifestation, redeem it. All this is implicit in the sign of the Virgin and its labour. In *The Secret Doctrine* is a clear statement of the whole message of this sign: "Matter is the vehicle for the manifestation of soul on this turn of the spiral; and soul is the vehicle on a higher turn of the spiral for the manifestation of spirit, and these three are a trinity synthesised by Life which pervades them all".

The Constellations and Stars

The three constellations in close proximity to that of Virgo are: *Coma Berenice,* the mother of the form only; the Centaur; the man riding upon a horse or the horse with a man's head and torso, representing the human being, for man is an animal plus a god. This is the lowest of the constellations and it is notable that Hercules, though he had passed through five Gates, failed at the sixth Gate, and had to begin again at the bottom, and make reparation for his lack of love and understanding. It often happens to advanced disciples. The third constellation holding promise of the future is *Bootes*, "the one who is coming", the saviour in Pisces who frees humanity from subservience to the form.

Virgo itself is a cup-shaped constellation with three main stars outlining it, the cup of communion, of which the Christ said "Drink ye all of it"; in its highest meaning the Holy Grail. The brightest star is *Spica,* which means "the ear of corn". Christ was born in Bethlehem, which means "the house of bread". We say, "Give us this day our daily bread," manna, bread from heaven, or the bread and wine of the communion. Ever this symbology of bread runs through the Old and New Testaments, and today our great economic problem still remains to furnish bread, a symbol of food, to a hungry world: bread for

the body and bread for those who hunger and thirst a̱ṯ̱_ _
eousness. All this as part of the nurturing function of the mother
of the world, who nourishes the form and also the Christ-consciousness latent in the form.

The Mutable Cross and the Planetary Rulers

Virgo is one of the arms of the mutable cross, with its opposite sign of Pisces, and the airy Gemini and fiery Sagittarius
completing the four arms. It is the common cross of those who
have probationary status. Its description is as follows: "The mutable cross is the cross of the Holy Spirit, of the third person of
the Christian trinity, as it organises substance and evokes sensitive response from substance itself". (Note the beautiful correlation of this statement with the fact that the Holy Spirit
overshadowed Mary.) On this cross the man reaches the stage
of *acquiescence and aspiration,* and so prepares himself for the
fixed cross of discipleship. It is notable that "the mutable cross
of the personality dedicates the man who is crucified thereon to
material ends in order that he may learn eventually their divine
use". "The sin against the Holy Ghost" has been the subject of
much morbid wondering. The Tibetan states: "The misuse of
substance and the prostitution of matter to evil ends is a sin
against the Holy Ghost". It was this sin, the greatest of his whole
pilgrimage, that Hercules committed in Virgo, when he did not
understand that the queen of the Amazons was to be redeemed
by unity, not killed. Over and over again the Tibetan emphasises
the fact that it is "through the medium of humanity that a consummation of 'light' effectiveness will be produced which will
make possible the expression of the whole". We still make the
mistake of Hercules, when we forget that the triangle of the Trinity is an equilateral triangle, all angles of equal importance, to
the working out of the Plan. (*Esoteric Astrology,* pp. 558 et seq.)
It is in Virgo, after complete individualisation in Leo, that the
first step toward the union of spirit and matter is made, "the subordination of the form life to the will of the indwelling Christ".

The three rulers of the sign Virgo definitely relate it to eight other signs, as has been noted, making it the outstanding sign of synthesis. Including Virgo itself, we have nine signs or energies inter-playing, the number of the months of gestation of the human embryo. Again "as above so below".

The orthodox ruler of the sign is Mercury, "the versatile energy of the son of mind, the soul", the intermediary between the Father and Mother. The esoteric ruler is the moon, veiling Vulcan. The moon rules the form and we are again reminded that it is the will of God to manifest through the form. Vulcan is an expression of first ray energy, while the moon exerts fourth ray energy; Jupiter is the hierarchical ruler representing the second creative Hierarchy (divine builders of earth's planetary manifestation), and brings in second ray energy.

The Tibetan points out that Mercury, Saturn and Venus rule the three decanates and he reminds us that when a man is on the reversed wheel of the disciple (counterclockwise) he will enter the sign through the influence of Venus, while the average man will enter under the rulership of Mercury. This is an example of how we may misinterpret a horoscope if we do not know the status of evolution of the native. Mundane astrology, without synthesis, may be very misleading and superficial. Alice Bailey was wont to say, with a twinkle in her eye, to a novice who exclaimed how exactly his chart was working out: "That is too bad, if you were living above the solar plexus, your personality chart would not work out so exactly". The chart of the soul will be used in the astrology of the future; not the chart of the personality. This warning is covered in a positive statement by the Tibetan: "The basis of the astrological sciences is the emanation, transmission, and reception of energies and their transmutation into forces by the receiving entity". This defines clearly what should be our attitude at full moon meditations and our use of individual horoscopes. "The point I seek to make here", says the Tibetan, "is that it is all a question of developed reception and sensitivity".

Significance of the Sign and its Polar Opposite

In the Mermaid, the fish goddess, we have the symbol of the at-one-ment of Virgo with its opposite sign Pisces. Always there is the duality, inherent in us and in the solar system; the second ray of the sun itself being a duality, Love-Wisdom. The lesson for the Virgo native, as stated by Dane Rudhyar in *Gifts of the Spirit,* is to have "a clear realisation that no truth is complete or even real which does not include its opposite, and all that occurs in between". Reminding one again that eight energies play through Virgo, that it is a sign of synthesis, Rudhyar states that transfiguration is required rather than transformation.

The three virtues demanded are tolerance, compassion and charity; one grows by becoming ever more inclusive. One of the most serviceable interpretations given is this comment on tolerance, the true nature of tolerance, which mostly as practised has a tinge of superiority and condescension. Rudhyar says: "Real tolerance goes far deeper than such an attitude of 'live and let live,' which is often not without a taint of smugness and self-centred indifference to everything but one's own truth . . .It means etymologically 'to bear.' To bear what? The burden of the necessity for change and growth . . .The Virgo's typical preoccupation with details of work, with technique, with health and hygiene, with analytical vivisection of himself and others, is actually a focalisation on the negative values of crisis". If the crisis in Virgo is positively met then, "the substance of consciousness itself is renewed and with this renewal, undertoning it, goes necessarily a re-statement of purpose".

For Pisces, the opposite pole, the keynote given is courage, and the Piscean temperament is called a battlefield, for its message is "liberation", and liberty must be fought for and earned, it cannot be a gift. The climax reads: "All conflicts are absolved, all transitions are resolved into Christ births", which is the climax of the birth of the latent Christ-consciousness in Virgo.

Keynotes

The heights and the depths of this sixth labour are clearly indicated in the keynotes of the sign: On the ordinary wheel the command goes forth in the following words, which constitute the activity of Virgo: "And the word said, 'let matter reign.' Later; upon the wheel of the disciple, the voice emerges from the Virgin herself, and she says: "I am the mother and the child. I, God, I, matter am". The Tibetan adds: "Ponder upon the beauty of this synthesis and teaching and know that you yourself have said the first word as the soul, descending into the womb of time and space in a far and distant time. The time has now come when you can, if you so choose, proclaim your identity with both divine aspects, matter and spirit, the mother and the child". (*Esoteric Astrology,* pp. 284-5). The first synthesising keynote is: "Christ in you, the hope of glory".

LABOUR VII.

THE CAPTURE OF THE ERYMANTHIAN BOAR
(Libra, September 22nd-October 21st)

The Myth

The great Presiding One, within the Council Chamber of the Lord, pondered the nature of the son of man who is likewise a son of God. He thought on what was needed to make him still more like unto his Father. "Another labour must be carried out. Balance he needs, and judgment sound, and preparation for a major test and future service to the race of men. For this, let him prepare with care". And the Teacher; noting on his tablets the purpose of the coming test, went forth and spoke to Hercules. "Go forth, my son, and capture the wild boar; salvage a ravaged country, yet take the time to eat". And Hercules went forth.

And Hercules, who is a son of man and yet a son of God, passed through the seventh Gate. The power of the seventh sign passed through him. He knew not that he faced a dual test, the test of friendship rare and the test of courage unafraid. The Teacher had instructed him to seek a boar, and Apollo gave to him a brand-new bow to use. Quoth Hercules: "I will not take it with me on the way, for fear I kill. At my last labour; upon the shores of the great sea, I slew and killed. This time I slaughter not. I leave the bow".

And so unarmed, save with his trusty club, he climbed the mountain steep, seeking the boar, and seeing sights, on every hand, of fear and terror. Higher and higher still he climbed. And then he met a friend. Upon the way, he met with Pholos, one of a group of centaurs, known unto the gods. They stopped and talked and for a time Hercules forgot the object of his search. And Pholos called to Hercules, inviting him to broach a cask of wine, which was not his, nor yet belonged to Pholos. Unto the group of centaurs, this great cask belonged, and from the gods, who dowered them with the cask, had come the word that never must the cask be broached, save when the centaurs met and all were present. It belonged unto the group.

But Hercules and Pholos opened it in the absence of their brothers, calling to Cherion, another centaur wise, to come and share their revels. This he did, and all the three together drank, and feasted and caroused and made much noise. This noise the other centaurs heard from distant points.

In wrath they came, and a fierce battle then took place and in spite of resolutions wise, again the son of man, who was a son of God, became the messenger of death and slew his friends, the centaurs twain with whom he earlier had drunk. And, whilst the other centaurs sorrowed with lamentations loud, Hercules escaped again into the mountains high, and again renewed his search.

* * *

Up to the limits of the snow he went, following the tracks of the fierce boar; up to the heights and bitter cold he followed it, and yet he saw it not. And night was drawing on, and one by one the stars came out, and still the boar outdistanced him. Hercules pondered on his task and sought within himself for subtle skill. He set a snare with skill, and wisely hid, and then he waited in a shadow dark for the coming of the boar. And hour by hour went by, and still he waited till the dawn drew near. Out from its lair the boar emerged, seeking for food, driven by ancient hunger. And in the shadows near the snare waited the son of man. Into the snare the boar fell and in due time Hercules released the savage beast making it the prisoner of his skill. He wrestled with the boar and mastered it, and made it do the thing he said, and go the. way that he desired.

Down from the snowy summit of the mountain high came Hercules, rejoicing on the way, driving before him, on the downward way, the fierce though tamed boar. By the hind legs twain, he drove the boar, and all upon the mountain laughed to see the sight. And all who met the son of man, who is the son of God, singing and dancing on the way, laughed too to see the progress of the two. And all within the city laughed to see the selfsame sight, the staggering, weary boar and the laughing, singing man.

Thus Hercules performed his seventh labour and returned unto the Teacher of his life.

And the great Presiding One within the Council Chamber of the Lord remarked: "The lesson of true balance hath been learnt. A lesson still remains. At the ninth Gate again, the centaur must be met and known and rightly understood".

And the Teacher said: "The seventh labour is completed, the seventh Gate passed. Ponder upon the lessons of the past; reflect upon the tests, my son. Twice have you slain that which you should love. Learn why". And Hercules stayed within the city gates and there prepared for that which later should befall, the test supreme.

THE TIBETAN.

Prologue

"The Mythus is the undisclosed thought of the soul". (*Isis Unveiled*)

Libra presents us with many paradoxes, and marked extremes, depending on whether one is on the clock-wise turn of the zodiac, or on the reversed path, the disciple who has turned, consciously, to the evolutionary path, the way homeward. It is said to be one of the most difficult signs to understand. It is the first sign that has neither a human nor an animal symbol, except that holding the balance stands the figure of Justice–a blinded woman, blinded perhaps to the outward objective sight, that the inner intuitive sight might divine where justice lies.

It is an interlude, we are told, comparable to the quiet listening in meditation; a time of assessment of the past. Again, strangely, the average man approaches Libra through the drastic test of Scorpio, while the more evolved man enters into the Libra test from the sign of Virgo, with the Christ consciousness stirring in his heart and mind. Think how different will be the experiences of these two men in Libra. In one case the balance will swing wildly up and down; in the other balance will be approached, or achieved, between matter and spirit, and all lesser pairs of opposites.

At this point we begin to see why, in this quiet sign, we meet with the problems of sex and money, both good servants and bad masters, according to the use made of them. Sex is a sacrament, at-one-ment of male and female, for the production of forms, for the carrying on of evolving life. Money is a means of exchange, of sharing at a distance, if not loved and held for itself alone, the gold of the miser, or the gold of the loving, giving heart.

The balance of the pairs of opposites (*Esoteric Astrology,* p. 250) is sharply defined. The balance may swing from bias and prejudice to justice or judgment; from dull stupidity to enthusiastic wisdom. How unusual and delightful a combination of words is that. In common parlance we symbolise wisdom by the rather stupid, blinking owl, and those who think themselves wise are too often full of solemnity and a bit stodgy, but wisdom should be "enthusiastic". Something to ponder, that. And there may be intrigue, the winding ways of man-made laws invite it; or there is straightforward conduct, and the Libran may be characterised by materialistic or by spiritual attitudes. Over and over again on this journey round, the constellations are all harmonious, good and for a purpose; it is our receptivity and use of them that determines what we manifest. It correlates with painful exactness the impressions gained by the casual tourist, and the man who goes and lives for a while in a country, and really knows its people. Sometimes one thinks that an intelligence test should be given before a visa is issued. Such wild ideas, for instance, are brought back by people who have spent a few days in Paris and think they then know France.

And in this stately sign of balance and justice and the law we find that the test ends in a burst of laughter, the only labour that does. Down from the mountain came Hercules, trundling the boar like a wheelbarrow, singing and laughing, and all onlookers laughed with him. How delightful; and this despite the fact that again Hercules made a dire mistake. The Teacher had told him to "take time to eat", but Hercules took time for a drunken orgy with two wise old centaur friends. And take note that they broached the cask of wine which was to be opened only by and for the group. A whole sermon could be preached on that point and also on the fact that, while Hercules took every precaution not to kill the boar, he ended by killing two friends. Thus does temptation come up behind us when we think we have cleared the path before us of pitfalls. But then the wise Teacher, when assessing the labour, passed lightly over the brawl, to which all had contributed, merely saying, "Ponder upon the lessons of the past" (Libra's assessment). "Twice have you slain that which you should love. Learn why". That is all; and we are reminded that the personality remains outside the ashram (our teachers see only whatever light we bear). There is no special praise, Hercules just passed, not *cum laude;* but the seventh labour was declared complete and the seventh Gate passed. Justice with mercy. "If Thou O God wilt be extreme to mark what is done amiss, O Lord who may abide it?"

Reflections of a Libran
    Before Hercules captured the Erymanthian boar, he sat at the table of Pholos and drank heady wine. At this time he was

the soul of conviviality, seeking and finding pleasure. For Hercules, as for all who assume the labour that must be performed in Libra, the fumes of pleasure must be dissipated before the greater task of self-mastery, i.e., the capturing of the boar, can be undertaken.

It is to be noted that the quaffing of the wine by Hercules leads to a tragedy, the death of Pholos. This sudden interjection of catastrophe into the pleasure-seeking existence of the Libran, harsh though the experience may be, is a necessity for the growth of the soul. Without such tragedies, the potentialities of Libra remain dormant. The Libran sets out upon his journey in winter, a time of bleakness when the personality life has lost its allure.

Hercules does not use brute force in taking the boar captive. He sets a trap, waits and allows the beast to trap itself. When the boar flounders in the snowdrifts, Hercules seizes his opportunity. It is curiously Libran to avoid a direct encounter, and not to expend more force than is necessary. He seeks to achieve his ends gently, not coercively.

We are told that Hercules seizes the hind legs of the boar, and compels the beast to walk down the mountainside on its front legs, and that this spectacle excites the laughter of all who witness it. In this incident we observe the Libran's ability to find unusual solutions, and to perceive the value of the incongruous.

Matters of great consequence in the history of mankind are determined by unusual approaches to common problems. For example, a Tartar chieftain started a great fire behind his own troops, thus forcing them to press forward with such desperate vigour that no enemy could withstand them. Again, when Hannibal sent his elephants against Scipio, the latter ordered soldiers to blow trumpets into the ears of the animals; confused and frightened by the noise, the elephants stampeded, and killed many of Hannibal's men.

The perception of incongruities is one of the greatest weapons given to mankind in its perpetual fight against glamour.

It is the source of the laughter that explodes pretence and destroys outmoded institutions.

This is the only labor that ends in a burst of laughter. Not only does Hercules perform the task assigned; he makes the ferocious boar an object of ridicule. By a slightly altered perspective, many of the terrifying experiences of life may be transformed by a beneficent sense of humour. Much of what people regard with grave and serious earnestness has decidedly ridiculous overtones.

The graphic description of Hercules driving the boar by its hind legs is a symbolic representation of the soul directing the ungainly body. This relationship in which each aspect achieves due importance is characteristic of the more highly organized Libran. Thus is the principle of balance observed.

The Libran goes about weighing and balancing all things. This attitude frequently makes him appear hesitant and indecisive. Knowing that there are innumerable gradations between black and white, he is seldom inclined to be an extremist. He knows that those who are regarded as pillars of society may be Pharisees, and the unostentatious and humble, the salt of the earth; that those who protest their excellence most vehemently may be the least meritorious; that the worldly-wise may act like fools, and fools may stumble upon treasures; that the judgments of the world may be reversed by a higher court; that truth may walk the earth in many an unlikely guise.

The quest for truth, then, becomes changed into the development of discrimination. In a sense, truth does not exist for human beings, for all truths are but fractional parts of greater wholes. The search for these more inclusive concepts is of more importance than the insistence upon an isolated fragment of a narrow, separate segment.

Like a busy spider, the Libran is perpetually spinning threads of relationships, creating a sensitive network of meanings. The result of such activity is synthesis. Between the concrete and the abstract he stands, trying to relate the two. Always there is a discrepancy, always the gap between the end envisioned and the goal achieved; and yet, the web glows luminously and assumes a pattern of intricate beauty.

Halfway between heaven and earth the Libran waits. Looking above, he sees the vision, the golden dawn gilding a snow-capped mountaintop; gazing downwards, he beholds the sloughs and the mire through which the sons of men pass. On the one hand, he cognises high ideals; on the other; he perceives them repudiated. At this midway point he must stand and work. If he rises towards the ideal world, he loses touch with common things; if he descends to the level of materialistic activity, he loses the precious perceptions that are the mainspring of his being. Between these two worlds he is poised in order that he might gain understanding; an understanding that includes the highest and the lowest, the good and the bad, the lofty and the insignificant. This is compassion.

The knowledge gained brings disillusionment. Peering into human hearts, he perceives the obscure shadows, and the sediment of strange passions therein. He discovers the base methods by means of which persons of consequence establish their success, the dark spots in the lives of reputable men, the clever ways by which they evade the promptings of conscience. He observes the budding ideas which are frost-bitten at the first temptation. He contemplates the long onward march of the human race, with its sporadic achievements and its multifarious failings.

What is the result of such reflections? First of all, the glamours that so often chain a man to earth are substantially weakened. He becomes aware that man lives in a swirling mist of illusion, clinging to life as an end in itself, often fleeing from truth as from a catastrophe. This description of shortcomings does not mean that human goodness is overlooked; without a sufficient measure of it, the world could not endure.

The Libran is not at all sure he cares to take part in the aggressive struggle to make a living, and to push his way for-

ward belligerently to a place of power and prestige
Were he concerned about himself alone, he would proba͟
treat to a library, and spend his days there. However, other
human beings also exist and they have claims upon him. The
motive of service thus takes root in his life, a sense of service
based on a realistic appraisal of human nature. Actually, it is
very difficult to serve the incredible species called man. Inform
a man of a truth that would, if accepted, alter his stereotyped
way of life, and he will as like as not condemn you as a radical;
reason with him, and he will stubbornly insist on the primacy
of his instincts; on the other hand, display indifference to his
plight, and he will denounce you for being callous to his sufferings. Whoever would serve the human race must be prepared
for misunderstanding, misinterpretation, and the perversity that
upholds the opposite of what is said.

The Libran is not inclined to be either a zealot or a tyrant.
Seeking to persuade rather than to compel, he understands the
art of spiritual compromise; this involves a willingness to yield
on all non-essential points, and an understanding that heaven
is reached by a series of separate steps rather than by a single
salvational leap. Serving others requires a just appraisal of their
capacities; to expect from them what they are incapable of giving is both unwise and frustrating. The help given to a person
must find expression within the framework of his limitations.
If this is not done, the aid may prove an impediment. A careful
distinction must be made between too much aid and too little;
if too much is given, the individual will not be encouraged to
use his own resources, whereas too little may cause him to sink
in a sea of despair. In other words, the help given must be care-
fully suited to the needs of the individual involved. In many
cases, help would only be an encumbrance; therefore, it is often
better to allow a person to fashion his spiritual certainties out
of his own bitter conflicts.

The constant weighing and measuring so characteristic of
Libra have one aim; the establishment of equilibrium. The

world is upheld by equilibrium, and this the Libran understands. As a matter of fact, the laws of karma may be considered as equilibrising activities that prevent the continuance of an unbalanced condition. The catastrophes that befall a man are meant, not to punish, but to restore equilibrium in his nature. He who establishes equilibrium in his own life will not be obliged to have it imposed upon him by harsh, bludgeoning circumstance. The scales of Libra are easily tipped on either side, but the mid-point on which the balance rests remains unchanged. This is the point of equilibrium, the secure retreat which the fluctuating shadows of earthly upheavals and catastrophes can never menace.

It should be pointed out that equilibrium, as here conceived, is a dynamic rather than a static condition. A balanced system of energies would be a more adequate definition; phrased differently, it might be called an ordered arrangement of energies directed and controlled by an over-arching will-to-good. The fully developed man, or initiate, might perhaps be described in such terms also.

In the midst of dissonance, the Libran cherishes the dream of harmony; in the far country, he remembers his Father's house. In memory thereof, he seeks to be a point of peace in a sea of clashing forces. That is the goal, but not always the achievement. However, this longing for harmony strengthens in him the desire to be a peacemaker. He can usually understand both sides of an issue, and this ability serves him well as a mediator and arbitrator.

The energies he employs are persuasion, courtesy, and co-operation; when these fail, he disdains harsher methods. He is naturally inclined towards group work, and is attracted by all programmes of action that promote brotherhood and unity.

There is a strongly feminine element in the Libran, and this is natural, since Venus rules the zodiacal sign. The hard, driving thrust of modern life is too aggressively masculine; the softer grace and artistic beauty of the feminine component should act as a complementary influence. The Libran instinctively understands this. He knows that masculine assertiveness must be modified by the subtler savour of feminine sweetness; that yielding water will outlast implacable stone and rigid steel.

When the Libran has assimilated the soft harmonies of Venus, he begins to respond to another vibration, that of Uranus. The statement in the Bible which describes this impulse is expressed in the words, "Behold, I make all things new". The old forms are understood to be chains and shackles. They must be discarded. The broom of God must sweep away the debris of the ages in order that the high ideals of brotherhood and unity may be incorporated into the very structure of our institutions, that the lives men lead may reflect the divine image that is indelibly imprinted in their essential being. Yet, this revolutionary change is not to be accomplished by a re-arrangement of outer shapes, forms, or institutions; it must originate within the human mind, in the silence of a man's heart, when he turns towards the light that shines upon him from the residue of immortality dwelling in him. The Libran sets out to re-make himself, knowing that this is his first step towards the re-making of the world.

The Rulers of Libra and Its Opposite Sign

The opposite sign of Libra, with which at-one-ment must be made, is Aries whose exoteric ruler is Mars, while the ruler of Libra is Venus. Exoterically, therefore, there must be at-one-ment between the Will and the higher mind, expressing itself through desire or love according to the status of evolution. The esoteric ruler of Libra is Uranus, and Saturn in this sign is the ruler of that "stupendous creative Hierarchy" which forms part of the third aspect of divinity. It is for this reason that Libra is closely connected with, and explains the third aspect of the Godhead and hence it is a governing sign and a major determining factor where law, sex and money are concerned. The Tibetan further states that, "If students will make a careful study of these three: law, first aspect; relation between the pairs of opposites (sex), second aspect; and concretised energy, called money, third aspect, as they express themselves today and as they can express themselves in the future, they will have a picture of physical human achievement and of future spiritual expression which will be instructive and most worthwhile. The whole process is accounted for by the activity of the three rulers of Libra: Venus, Uranus and Saturn".

Condensation, *Esoteric Astrology,* p. 243 et seq.

Peculiar beauty emerges when considering the keynotes of Aries and Libra as given by Dane Rudhyar in *Gifts of the Spirit.* The note for Libra is "ease", but it is far from the ease of luxurious comfort. The author defines it as "an expression of totally accepted relatedness, be it with an object, a situation or a person . . . Men can only be free from nature by fulfilling nature; by fulfilling it with ease, with elegance.

"By elegance we mean that quality which the mathematician has in mind when he speaks of 'the elegant solution of a mathematical problem,' a solution which moves on with extreme ease, with the utmost simplicity of means, with a minimum of intermediary steps, with inherent logic. A redwood tree is likewise the elegant solution of the problem contained in the seed; a perfectly easy and logical development of the potentialities inherent in this seed.

"Natural growth of inherent potentialities, ease and logic of development, elegance of unfoldment; these are jewels of the art of living; these are the tests of mastery".

Let your mind rest in contemplation of these beautiful words. It is difficult to imagine a more refreshing concept of growth, a growth which unfolds from within as a flower opens, instead of with stress and anxious strain. Here we might note that Libra represents the vegetable kingdom, sex and natural affinity. In that kingdom three rays are said to be vibrating in unison. This results in service, beauty, colour and fragrance. Rudhyar's words are not mystical poetry; they are rooted in biological fact, where also creative energy, God immanent, is at work.

Turning to Aries, we find that the keynote is "adaptability", which indicates a method by which the "ease" of Libra may be obtained. We all know of men and women, in history and about us now, who move with poise and power amidst tragic happenings. And what an awesome, inspiring sight it is. We find adaptability also in the camouflage of the animal kingdom, in the colouring of birds and beasts which helps to protect their lives. Man in dangerous circumstances has an equal need for camouflage, in his case, for increased adaptability. This immediately raises a query as to the dangers of compromise, the deserting of principle for safety. But just as the Tibetan has told us that "spiritual compromise" may be a recognition of time and evolution, not involving any treachery to the goal, so we read the following by Rudhyar:

> "This type of social adaptation should not be such as to divert or muddy the flow of the release of power. It should not alter the quality of the projected images, or cloud the vision they convey . . . This is a difficult task of discrimination. To be adaptable, yet to retain the purity and total integrity of one's vision and one's ideal; to accept detours, yet not lose the direction of the goal; to be understandable and acceptable to those who need the spiritual arousal, yet not distort or lower the character of the message; to use the values born of the past, yet not sell short the future to the uncertain present; to be kind to men, yet uncompromisingly true to the spirit – such are the problems that the Aries person will constantly meet, in one form or another.
>
> The individual who is consecrated and true to the spirit acts *as* the spirit in terms of human needs". (Ease and adaptability: Libra at-one with its opposite sign, Aries.)

The Constellations and the Stars

There are three constellations in Libra, all of special interest. First there is the southern cross that has never been seen in the Occident since the time of the Crucifixion, when it was seen at Jerusalem. Now the cross is receding. Let us try to grasp the dramatic presentation in this great symbol. Four bright stars make up this cross; four; the number of the matter aspect of man, the quaternary. The southern cross, the quaternary, is receding. The same symbolism is seen in Gemini, with *Castor* and *Pollux*. *Pollux*, symbolising immortality, is growing brighter and *Castor*, mortality, is growing dimmer. The cross is receding, and this promise is in Libra, called the open door to Shamballa, the sign in which there is found "the narrow, razor-edged path" which leads the man into the kingdom of the soul.

The second constellation is that of *Lupus*, the wolf. Down the ages, the wolf's head has been the symbol of the initiate. But it is a dying wolf, and the wolf-nature that has devoured the soul nature until now is symbolised as dying out, for as man achieves balance the activity and power of the wolf dies out.

The third is the *Corona*, the crown held before man working in Libra. The symbol is based on the story of Ariadne, the mother aspect, who was given a crown of seven stars by Bacchus, symbol of the second aspect of divinity which glorifies matter by making it the expression of the divine mind. (From A.A.B.).

As with all of Libra, interpretations and understanding of the constellations are difficult, but provocative of thought. If the data seems meagre and vague it is perhaps again representative of Libran interlude, which one of the Masters of the Wisdom has called "the master of no-man's land". So we can but ponder, remembering how the wolf appears as the animal that suckled Romulus and Remus; and was the fierce animal which Saint Francis of Assisi tamed by his love for it, and sense of oneness with it.

Some highlights from the lecture by A.A.B.

In Libra we have the man who does not speak, symbolic of the interlude of silence in the life of Jesus. Between the ages of 12 and 30, we hear naught of him. These were years of silence, whether spent among the Essenes in Egypt or in the carpenter's shop, in which that great son of God balanced spirit and matter and prepared for his ministry as a son of man who was also a son of God – demonstrably. The great revelation to my mind is not that we are spirit, but that all is God in manifestation; it is all energy in different categories. Christ was the perfect expression of divinity in form. He balanced spirit and matter perfectly. That is the work we all have to do. . .

The two good centaurs that Hercules killed are known as Cherion (good thought) and Pholos (bodily strength). This test was to show control of the emotional, astral, desire nature, in whatever form it may take; and it is all the more powerful the more advanced a human being is. You cannot control or guide the desire nature by physical strength or by thought alone. You may succeed for a time and then it surges back up in you again. The only answer is to take the boar of desire up into the high mountains. It is on mountain tops that all the great revelations occur, where the mists of the valley disappear and illumination comes. . .

Libra is an air sign and is on the cardinal cross which will govern the next solar system and in this system governs the path of initiation, which is trodden by the flower of the race (*Esoteric Astrology,* p. 279). Again the mystery veils so that we find the sign difficult to understand. But the keynotes of the sign are clear and plain: they speak straight to the heart and without obscurity. To the average man, with no developed spiritual consciousness, the word goes forth again and again throughout the eons: "And the Word said: let choice be made". The response eventually comes back as a result of the evolutionary process and from the soul. "I choose the way which leads between the two great lines of force". (*Ibid.* pp. 251, 261).

LABOUR VIII.

DESTROYING THE LERNAEAN HYDRA
(Scorpio, October 22-November 21)

The Myth*

The great Presiding One, enrobed in radiant calm, said but a single word. The Teacher heard the golden command, and summoned Hercules, the son of God who was also the son of man.

"The light now shines on Gate the eighth", the Teacher said. "In ancient Argos a drought occurred. Amymone besought the aid of Neptune. He bade her strike a rock, and when she did, out-gushed three crystal streams; but soon a hydra made his dwelling there.

"Beside the River Amymone, the festering swamp of Lerna stands. Within this noisome bog the monstrous hydra lies, a plague upon the countryside. Nine heads this creature has, and one of them is immortal. Prepare to battle with this loathsome beast. Think not that common means will serve; destroy one head, two grow apace". Expectantly Hercules waited.

"One word of counsel only I may give", the Teacher said. "We rise by kneeling; we conquer by surrendering; we gain by giving up. Go forth, O son of God and son of man, and conquer". Through Gate the eighth, then, Hercules passed.

The stagnant swamp of Lerna was a blot dismaying all who came within its confines. Its stench polluted all the atmosphere

---

*Beginning with Scorpio the statement of the myth will be written by Dr. Francis Merchant, as no further copy by the Tibetan was found among the papers of A.A.B. He has used the best available material for the details of the story casting it in the iambic cadence of The Old Commentary. Other material by A.A.B. is used as before, with some necessary condensations and rewriting.

within a space of seven miles. When Hercules approached, he had to pause, for the smell alone well-nigh overcame him. The oozing quicksands were a hazard, and more than once Hercules quickly withdrew his foot lest he be sucked downward by the yielding earth.

At length he found the lair where dwelt the monstrous beast. Within a cavern of perpetual night, the hydra lay concealed. By day and night Hercules haunted the treacherous fen, awaiting a propitious time when the beast would sally forth. In vain he watched. The monster stayed within its fetid den.

Resorting to a stratagem, Hercules dipped his arrows in burning pitch, and rained them straight into the yawning cavern where dwelt the hideous beast. A stirring and commotion thereupon ensued.

The hydra, its nine angry heads breathing flame, emerged. Its scaly tail lashed furiously the water and the mud, bespattering Hercules. Three fathoms high the monster stood, a thing of ugliness that looked as if it had been made of all the foulest thoughts conceived since time began.

The hydra sprang at Hercules and sought to coil about his feet. He stepped aside and dealt it such a crushing blow that one of its heads was immediately disservered. No sooner had this horrid head fallen into the bog than two grew in its place. Again and again Hercules attacked the raging monster, but it grew stronger, not weaker, with each assault.

Then Hercules remembered that his Teacher had said, "we rise by kneeling". Casting aside his club, Hercules knelt, grasped the hydra with his bare hands, and raised it aloft. Suspended in mid-air, its strength diminished. On his knees, then, he held the hydra high above him, that purifying air and light might have their due effect. The monster, strong in darkness and in sloughy mud, soon lost its power when the rays of the sun and the touch of the wind fell on it.

Convulsively it strove, a shudder passing through its loathsome frame. Fainter and fainter grew its struggles till the victory was won. The nine heads drooped, then with gasping mouths and glazing eyes fell limply forward. But only when they lifeless lay did Hercules perceive the mystic head that was immortal.

Then Hercules cut off the hydra's one immortal head and buried it, still fiercely hissing, beneath a rock.

Returning, Hercules stood before his Teacher. "The victory is won", the Teacher said. "The Light that shines at Gate the eighth is now blended with your own."

Francis Merchant.

Introduction

Again we find variations in the versions of the myth and we have no longer the myth statement by the Tibetan to guide us. The story that the ninth head was the immortal head seems ruled out by the Tibetan's plain statement that there were three times three, or nine tests. The version used by Francis Merchant in the myth seems more accurate, namely that nine heads were destroyed and then the mystical, immortal head appeared. Further, the statement that this great head was "buried under a rock", gives ground for much pondering. Perhaps the use of the phrase, "hidden under the rock of the will", is revealing. All versions state that it was so buried.

In some accounts it is stated that Hercules burned off the heads, and the divine fire would indeed be needed for this destruction. However, it is impossible to negate the powerful picture of the world disciple in this supreme test, sinking to his knees in humility and raising the monster (all the accumulated evils, mistakes, failures of his long past) into the air of the spirit, where by its very nature the hydra could not live, and so drooped and died. The use of the fire, in the preliminary effort, still keeps that symbol in the picture.

While sex, under the test of at-one-ment of opposites and the double rulership of Mars, has its special place, the over-emphasis of this one facet is not sufficiently inclusive. All pairs of opposites are to be at-oned in this great sign, an advanced sign of the integrated, conscious disciple; not a sordid one of the un-evolved man, as is often thought. Again, one must read care-fully and distinguish between people on the ordinary wheel and disciples on the reversed wheel. All of which is submitted for the pondering of the reader, not with authority.

Psychological Analysis of the Myth

Hercules was told to find the nine-headed hydra that lived in a stench-drenched bog. This monster has its subjective coun-terpart. It dwells within the caverns of the mind. In the murk and mud of unlit mental recesses, it flourishes.

Deeply lodged within the subterranean regions of the sub-conscious, now quiescent and now bursting forth in tumultuous frenzy, the beast establishes permanent residence. Its existence is not easily discovered. A long time passes before the individ-ual realises that he is nourishing and sustaining so fierce a crea-ture. The burning arrows of flaming aspiration must be discharged before its presence is revealed.

Fighting so formidable a foe is indeed a heroic task for a son of man even though he is also a son of God. Lop off one head, and another grows in its place. Every time a low desire or thought is overcome, others take its place.

Hercules does three things: he recognises the existence of the hydra, searches patiently for it, and finally destroys it. Dis-crimination is needed to recognise its existence; patience, to discover its lair; humility, to bring slimy fragments of the sub-conscious to the surface, and expose them to the light of wis-dom.

As long as Hercules fought in the bog, amid the mud, slime, and quicksand, he was unable to overcome the hydra. He had to raise the monster into the air; that is, translate his problem into another dimension, in order to solve it. In all humility, kneeling in the mud, he had to examine his dilemma in the light of wisdom and in the elevated atmosphere of searching thought. From these considerations we may gather that the answers to many of our problems come only when a new focus of attention is achieved, a new perspective established.

One of the hydra's heads is immortal, we are told. This would imply that every difficulty, however terrible it may appear to be, contains a jewel of great value. No attempt to dominate the lower nature and discover that jewel is ever futile.

The immortal head, dissevered from the hydra's body, is buried beneath a rock. This implies that the concentrated energy which creates a problem still remains, purified, redirected, and increased after victory has been gained. Such power must then be rightly controlled and channelled. Beneath the rock of persistent will, the immortal head becomes a source of power.

The Nine Heads of the Hydra

The task assigned to Hercules had nine facets. Each head of the hydra represents one of the problems that beset the courageous person who seeks to achieve mastery of himself. Three of these heads symbolise the appetites associated with sex, comfort and money. The second triune group concerns the passions of fear, hatred and desire for power. The last three heads represent the vices of the unillumined mind: pride, separativeness and cruelty.

See Esoteric Astrology, p. 205 et seq.

The dimensions of the task which Hercules undertook are thus plainly apparent. He had to learn the art of transmuting the energies that so frequently precipitate human beings into catastrophic tragedies. The nine forces which have wrought unspeakable havoc among the sons of men since the beginning of time had to be re-directed and transmuted.

Men today are still striving to achieve what Hercules succeeded in accomplishing. Problems arising out of the misuse of the energy known as sex engage our attention on every hand. The love of comfort, luxury and outer possessions still grows apace. The pursuit of money as an end instead of a means shrinks the lives of countless men and women. Thus, the task of destroying the first three heads continues to challenge the powers of mankind thousands of years after Hercules accomplished his extraordinary feat.

The three qualities of character that Hercules had to express were humility, courage and discrimination: humility, to see his plight objectively and recognise his shortcomings; courage, to attack the monster that lay coiled at the roots of his nature; discrimination, to discover a technique for dealing with his mortal foe.

Uncovering the cesspool of base desires and egotistical urges that fester in the subconscious nature has been the work of modern psychoanalysis. The latter technique brings the unsavoury data of repressed impulses to the surface, it is true, but often stops at that point. The individual realises that a monster lies concealed in the subterranean areas of consciousness, yet feels baffled and bewildered in trying to deal with this formidable enemy.

Hercules invokes a brighter light than that of the analysing mind. He seeks to raise his problem to a higher dimension, not to stir endlessly in the slough of the subconscious. Endeavouring to see his dilemma in the light of that wisdom which we name the soul, he confronts it from a new angle of vision. By so doing, he breaks the hydra's grip, and eventually subdues the beast.

Fighting the Hydra: Modern Version

A consideration of the nine problems that confront the person in this day and age who seeks to slay the hydra, should shed light on the strange forces at work in that keg of explosive, the human mind.

ex. Victorian prudishness and psychoanalytical pruri- ence are both undesirable. Sex is an energy. It can be inhibited, unrestrainedly exercised, or sublimated. Repression or inhibi- tion are no true solutions; promiscuity coarsens life, and makes a man a slave of a master passion. Sublimation involves the use of the energy of sex in creative endeavour.

The transmutation of human energies opens up a field of speculation and experiment. In physical science, the energy of motion can be transformed into electricity, and that of heat into movement. To what extent, then, can human energies be re-di- rected? First of all, the energy of matter, represented by food, is obviously used to produce that of motion. Can the impelling energy of the emotions analogously be re-channelled into the activity of thought? Can the energy of seething passions find expression as aspiration? Can the drives and compulsions of human nature be so transmuted that they become beneficent powers? Can the energy that produces thought be utilised as the power of synthesis that results in a sense of identification with all living things?

The experience of Hercules indicates that such possibilities exist, and that he who would subdue the hydra of the passions and the separative mind must solve problems of this nature.

2. *Comfort.* An eternal sense of dissatisfaction spurs man to ever greater heights of achievement. Comfort is often a brake upon such striving. Clogged down with possessions and blunted by the beguiling sense of comfort, the spirit wilts and fades. The prisoner of comfort sinks back in apathy, forgetting the struggles and trials that temper the keen blade of spiritual striv- ing. The will to search, the impelling drive to solve the mystery in the acorn of life, is alien to the narcissistic inclination to make comfort a central motive in life.

3. *Money.* The accumulation of money is a master passion that lies behind the activities of people and nations. Ethical and human values are disregarded in the mad endeavour to gather power-conferring gold. Inevitably, choices are determined by

money considerations rather than by spiritual convictions or ethical principles. The urge to accumulate wealth is insatiable. No matter how much a person may have, he still avidly craves more.

A crippling effect of this form of mental distortion is self-centredness. The individual suffering from this affliction too often wishes to receive everything and to give nothing. The state of the universe is determined for him by what he succeeds in acquiring. He regards himself as a terminal point, and acknowledges no responsibility to confer on others the benefits he himself has received.

Are not intellectual riches and spiritual treasure aspects of wealth that should claim our efforts? They may be shared with all, and he who gives away all he has, finds himself richer than he was before. The urge to acquire material goods may some day be transmuted into the desire to amass knowledge and the will to acquire the jewels of the spirit.

4. *Fear.* In countless ways the phantoms of fear torment the sons of men. These illusory shapes perplex and frighten them, acting as shackles on their feet and a millstone around their necks. Many people cower cravenly when haunted by the harrowing fears of ridicule, failure, the unknown, old age, chance and death.

Can these fears be eliminated? The experience of Hercules suggests that they can be overcome by raising consciousness to a higher point of integration. When a person's life is re-focused about a higher purpose, the threatening shadows of fear are pressed back to the periphery of thought. As long as the indeterminate monsters of fear prowl in the twilight of the subconscious, they will have the power to blanch the cheek and turn the heart to ice.

A soldier, intent on defeating the enemy, risks life itself. A mother, snatching her child from danger, forgets her own fears. The motorist, hurtling down a highway at breakneck speed, jeopardises life and limb for the sake of adventure. These persons have focused their attention above the point where fear is found. The spiritually-oriented individual has centred his thought at a level too rarefied for fear to reach.

5. *Hatred.* Hate is rooted in negation. It is the opposite of the desire for union. Raised to a higher dimension, hate is transmuted into the repudiation of all that is unreal. When hate is divested of all emotional content, it can become an energy that causes a man to reject the form for the sake of the life which animates it. Upon the lower arc, it is assuredly destructive; upon the higher, when thoroughly purified, it may be seen as the obverse side of love.

6. *Desire for power.* During the past few hundred years man has released the energy of power far more than that of love. The result is imbalance and disequilibrium. Power, when unrelated to love, is a corrupting force. Many tragedies in human relations result from the uncontrolled desire to dominate the lives of others, to prescribe and regulate their conduct. He who substitutes power considerations for ethical principles engenders perpetual strife. The high ideals that have served as beacons over the centuries, brotherhood, co-operation, idealism, glow dimly as long as power is the determining factor in society.

When transmuted, however, the will to power becomes the will to achieve and the will to sacrifice. The harsh, self-centred will is transformed into a distributing agent of beneficent gifts. Then, indeed, power serves love and love glorifies power.

7. *Pride.* The walls built by pride incarcerate a man more securely than prison bars. Fastened by the heavy chains of self-exalting thoughts, he looks at other human beings with condescension. Thus he weakens the link that binds all men together in indissoluble brotherhood. Setting himself apart, he steps further and further beyond the circle of human sympathies.

Hercules falls to his knees as he struggles with the hydra, symbolising in this posture the spirit of humility that must be attained. The exaltation of personality inclinations must be replaced by the expression of self-sacrificing tendencies.

8. *Separativeness.* The analytical mind divides and sub-divides, prizing the part above the whole. Greater emphasis is placed upon the indications of diversity than on the over-arching fact of unity. Such fragmented thinking militates against the impulse toward synthesis.

The separative attitude is more conscious of the differences between men than of the similarities; it conceives of religion as a series of antagonistic units rather than a single expression of spiritual impulse; it considers the opposition of classes in society to be more important than the common humanity that makes men brothers; it views the earth as a series of disparate nations, rather than as one world.

Hercules had to see the hydra as one monster, not a beast with nine different heads. As long as he sought to dissever the heads, one by one, he remained unsuccessful. When he finally dealt with it as a unit, he gained the victory.

9. *Cruelty.* The satisfaction men experience in hurting others is a testimony to the existence of evil tendencies that corrode the mind. Delight in causing suffering to our fellow men is a disease. This ugly head of the hydra must be destroyed once and for all before a man can declare himself to be humanised. Modern life offers many examples of brutality and wanton cruelty. In many families sensitive children are taunted, ridiculed and disparaged by those who refuse to take the trouble to understand them; husbands and wives are daily proclaiming to the world in divorce appeals that they are victims of mental torture; the courts and hospitals produce cumulative evidence of the irrational pleasure which human beings take in tormenting each other. "We do it for thrills", said a teenage gangster lately, "not for money".

When this monster cruelty is held high in the air in the light of reason and compassion, it loses its power. The task of translating the energy of cruelty into that of active compassion still remains. In two tests Hercules "killed" when he should have loved, but in Scorpio he achieved this transformation, rooting out of his own nature a tendency which would have crippled him in every future undertaking.

Such is the achievement of Hercules, psychologically speaking, in this labour. He has admitted light into the dark recesses of the subconscious, grappled with the monstrous forces that wallow in subliminal slime, and has overcome the enemies of his own household. A cleansing process has taken place, and Hercules is now ready to embark upon the next labour in which he will have to demonstrate his ability to control the powers and potencies of the mind.

Francis Merchant.

Applications to Life
Condensation of lecture by A.A.B.

Scorpio is the labour that from certain angles has engrossed us and will engross us for a long time because, unlike Hercules, we have not triumphed over the hydra. Most of us are occupied with the futile methods first employed by him in this test.

This primarily is humanity's problem, but individually we are so profoundly concerned with our own evolution that we forget the larger view. If ever we are going to climb the mountaintop in Capricorn we must lose sight of the personality and begin to function as souls.

In my highest moments I know theoretically what my attitude and actions should be, but I go muddling along. Why? Because of a fundamental law that everything in nature evolves sequentially, step by step, line upon line, precept upon precept. It might be a devastating experience if I so quickly cleared up my personality that the whole force of my soul could pour in. I would be swept off my feet by the power and light, the omniscience and omnipotence of my soul. I would not know what to do with what I had. That does not mean that all I have to do is sit back and let the law work, rest on my oars and evolution will carry me along until at some time I achieve. It does mean that at this time I am on the battlefield, Kurukshetra, and I am going to deal with this hydra in Scorpio, for it is this labour which is engrossing humanity today.

The true Scorpio test never takes place until one is co-ordinated, until one's mind, emotional nature and physical nature are functioning as a unit. Then the man passes into Scorpio where his equilibrium is upset and desire seems rampant when he had thought he had got rid of it. He is fluidic, and he had thought he was balanced. The mind which he was quite sure was beginning to control his personality does not seem to function. As we study Hercules, we see ourselves.

Remember that there are three things the disciple has to do in Scorpio. He has to demonstrate, not to the Hierarchy, not to the onlooker, but to himself, that he has overcome the great illusion; that matter, form, cannot hold him any longer. Hercules has to demonstrate to himself that form is simply a channel of expression whereby he contacts a great field of divine manifestation. From reading some books on religion one might come to the conclusion that form, emotion and mind are all evil, undesirable things, to be got rid of. To my mind, it is fundamental to grasp the thought that if I get rid of physical form I have no means of contacting one divine expression, because God is in my fellow man, in this physical, tangible world in which I live, and if I have no form, none of my five senses, I shut off from myself God in one form. The personality is not to be killed, not be stamped out; it is to be recognised as a triple channel of expression for three divine aspects. All depends upon whether we use that triple personality for selfish or divine ends. The great illusion is the utilisation of that personality for selfish ends. To sum up the whole story, in the sign Scorpio, the Self is determined to kill the little self in order to teach it the meaning of resurrection.

What is Death?

There are three death signs in the zodiac; three great deaths take place as we progress around the field of life. In Cancer, we have the death of the elemental being (namely, man) in order that the human being can come into existence. Right through the zodiac we can always say: "Here is death in order that..".

Always, death is an entrance into a fuller life, fuller experience, fuller realisation and scope. It is the death of the personality in order that the soul may take over the personality and express life through it. In Pisces we have the crucifixion, the death of a world saviour because he has perfectly fulfilled his function.

Death in astrology may mean many things. Perhaps it may mean that we are going to die. That is one interpretation. Perhaps we are going to die to an old emotion. It has passed away – "death". Some crystallised, long-held ideas, dogmas, that have governed our activities until now have simply come to an end and we wonder how we could possibly have thought as we did. That line of thought has died. It is valuable to get the big picture and learn to interpret it in the various aspects of the personality.

Scorpio, the Sign of Magic

Magic does not mean doing curious things: true magic is the expression of the soul through the medium of the form. Black magic is the use of form in order to gain what we want for the form. Black magic is unadulterated selfishness. White magic is use of the soul for purposes of human uplift, utilising the personality. Why is Scorpio the sign of magic? An ancient book says: "Virgo is the witch, she prepares the ingredients which are weighed in the balances in Libra, and in Scorpio the magical work is carried forward". In terms of the aspirant this means that in Virgo I discovered the Christ in myself, that down the ages my form nature has nurtured a Christ; in Libra I fluctuate between the pairs of opposites, form and the Christ nature, until I achieve balance and the Christ and matter are in a stage of equilibrium. In Scorpio I am tested as to which will triumph, the form or the Christ, the higher Self or the lower self, the real or the unreal, the true or the illusion. That is the underlying story of Scorpio.

The Constellations and the Stars

Taurus, which is the opposite of Scorpio, is the sign of desire expressed predominantly on the physical plane as sex. At the heart of Scorpio we find *Antares,* one of the four royal stars, a red star. Red is the colour of desire and this is the reddest star in the heavens; it symbolises that red of desire that underlies every manifestation of divine life.

In Gemini, in the gathering of the golden apples, Hercules also wrestled with *Antares*. Here again in Scorpio we are up against the red star. Why? Because the problem of humanity in this great solar system of ours is that of the attraction between the opposites (meaning desire). Always there is duality, that which is desired and the one who desires. Aquila, the eagle, is interchangeable with Scorpio. The eagle has much to do with the United States and the arrow of Sagittarius, the next sign, is also dominant in the seal of the United States. Aquila, the eagle, is the bird out of time and space and as Hercules struggles with the hydra he looks up, sees the eagle, and is reminded that he has come forth into incarnation and will fly back from whence he came.

There are three constellations connected with this sign which are tremendously interesting. First, there is *Serpens,* the serpent of illusion, the serpent we meet in *Genesis,* which deluded Eve. The second one is *Ophiuchus*, the man who wrestles with the serpent. The ancient zodiac portrays the serpent in the hands of this man. He seizes it with both hands and treads on its heart, which is the red star of desire. As he does this, he looks towards the constellation that we saw in Libra, the crown. So we have personality, symbolised by *Ophiuchus,* struggling with the serpent of illusion, with the crown held before him, towards which he aspires.

The third constellation is called *Hercules* and portrays the aspirant looking not at the crown but at the eagle, Aquila. Personality looks at the crown but says, "I am having such a difficult time, my environment is against me, my home conditions are difficult, but I will get a crown some day". Hercules, the disciple, is not concerned about the crown, he is looking at the eagle, the spirit aspect. He is occupied with that marvellous symbol of light emerging, which makes all victory possible.

Keep your eye on the eagle; call down fire; do not look at the ground; be centred in divinity.

Alice A. Bailey.

LABOUR IX.

KILLING THE STYMPHALIAN BIRDS
(Sagittarius, November 22nd-December 21st)

The Myth

Within the place of peace the Teacher stood, and spoke to Hercules. "O son of God who art also a son of man", the Teacher said, "the time has come to tread another way. At Gate the ninth you stand. Pass through and find the marsh of Stymphalus where dwell the birds that havoc wreak. Discover, then, the way to flush them from their long secure abode".

He paused a moment. "The flame that gleams beyond the mind reveals direction sure," he added. "The task awaits. Through Gate the ninth you now must go."

Forward, then, went Hercules, the son of man who was also the son of God.

For long he searched until he came to Stymphalus. Before him lay the fetid marsh. A multitude of birds cawed raucously, a chorus menacing and dissonant, as he approached.

At nearer view he saw the birds. Large and fierce and hideous they were. Each had an iron beak that was sharpened like a sword. The feathers, too, seemed like steel shafts and, falling, could cleave in twain the pates of weary travellers. Their talons matched their beaks in sharpness and in strength.

Three birds, perceiving Hercules, swooped down upon him. He stood his ground, and warded off attacks with the heavy club he bore. One bird he struck resoundingly upon the back; two feathers plummeted to earth and quivered as they plunged into yielding ground. At length the birds withdrew.

Before the marsh stood Hercules, and pondered how he might achieve the task assigned, how rid the place of these predacious birds.

By many means he sought to find a way. At first he tried to kill them with a quiverful of arrows. The few he slew were but a fraction of the many that remained. They rose in clouds so thick they hid the sun.

He thought of setting traps within the marsh. Nor boat nor human feet could traverse the bog.

Hercules paused. The words he then recalled of counsel given. "The flame that gleams beyond the mind reveals direction sure." Reflecting long, a method came to mind.

Two cymbals had he, large and brazen, that gave forth an unearthly screeching sound; a sound so piercing and so harsh it could affright the dead. To Hercules himself the sound was so intolerable, he covered both his ears with pads.

At twilight when the marsh was dense with countless birds, Hercules returned. The cymbals then he sharply clashed, again and yet again. A clangour and a din so strident then ensued that he himself could scarce endure the sound. Such ear-assaulting dissonance had not been heard in Stymphalus before.

Bewildered and disturbed by such a monstrous noise, the predatory birds rose in the air with wildly flapping brazen wings, and screeched in hoarse dismay. Utterly confused, the vast cloud of birds fled in frantic haste, never to return. Silence spread across the marsh. The horrid birds had disappeared. The soft gleam of a westering sun was seen as it flickered on the darkening landscape.

When Hercules returned, the Teacher greeted him: "The birds of slaughter have been driven off. The labour is achieved."

Francis Merchant.

Interpretation of the Labour
Edited Lecture by A.A.B., 1937

Sagittarius is to my mind most interesting because it has such a peculiar application to each one of us answering to the name "aspirant".

There are two words I want to see ruled out of the vocabulary of the occultist, "initiate" and "master". "Initiate" is delightfully separative, it is a pedestal word. "Master" has bred in the consciousness of people the feeling that there exist superhuman men who assume the attitude of directors or masters over their disciples; who tell them what to do and how to do it. No real adept has ever been known to do that.

I like the words "aspirant" and "disciple". Aspirant is a blanket word that covers us at every stage of our development. If you want a more technical word, use disciple; it is a hiding word, because an aspirant of the lowest degree is a disciple. The Christ himself is also a disciple. It does away with grades and classes and degrees and varied stages of evolution.

Where we stand on the ladder of evolution is our own private affair. The world will know what we are, when we have done the work that is outlined for us in this labour of Sagittarius.

We have already dealt with the stupendous sign Scorpio, in which Hercules demonstrated to himself the fact that he could no longer be taken in by the serpent of illusion. He was free from fear and glamour, from all that could beguile him. The vision could be seen.

Because Sagittarius is such a tremendously important sign I want to give you a brief resumé of what has happened up to the present time; it covers what lies behind us. I am assuming that each one of us is the one-pointed aspirant, the archer on the horse, going straight as an arrow to his goal.

It is interesting that the United States' standard shows the arrows of Sagittarius in the talons of an eagle, because Aquila is interchangeable astrologically with Sagittarius and is the symbol of the spirit manifesting through the soul, which the aspirant on the physical plane is one-pointedly seeking. There is prophecy in the United States standard, of the goal of this race when it is grown up, for it is within this race that there will emerge that group of aspirants, merging in their turn into a group of disciples, who will demonstrate to the planet the fact of the subjective world. That is the destiny of this race. It will be the achievement of all the races gathered together in the United States.

Let us narrow the story down to Hercules, the aspirant, and what he has done in each sign.

In Aries, Hercules began on the plane of the mind in his endeavour to capture the man-eating mares, and met with failure because he dealt with them in a personality way. He dealt with thought from the standpoint of personality; he did not work with his problem from the standpoint of the soul. In Sagittarius he slaughtered the man-eating birds. He was back again to the same problem on the plane of the mind where he demonstrated complete control of that which is the first thing the aspirant to initiation has to do. We control our thoughts and consequently control our words. There is no initiation for us until we do. In Aries he began to control thought.

In Taurus he worked down to the astral plane and came up against the problem of sex, the demonstration of the great law of attraction in the universe in its lowest aspect. He had fairly good success. He did control the bull and drove it into the city of the Cyclops.

In Gemini it began to dawn upon him that he was dual; he was engrossed with the problem of soul and body and how to co-ordinate them. That is why Gemini fluctuates in the early stages.

In Cancer he passed on to a certain amount of mass consciousness; he took form. That is a stage of human incarnation. With many, the fact that they are human beings with relationship to other human beings just does not enter into their consciousness at all. In Cancer, Hercules began to get that viewpoint. The moment you get that, you capture the timid doe of the intuition, and you begin to be intuitive, not psychic.

Then Hercules passed into that difficult sign Leo, where so many now are, and became a very forceful individual. He was sure he could do everything, he stood alone: a stage of power. At this stage you are going to rule men, and you begin by ruling them wrongly. You assert yourself too forcefully, and you think you are more important than you are. You have to get rid of the sense of "I am". That is the whole story of the life of the aspirant. You must become so identified with the real spiritual entity that lies back of all forms that you are not occupied with your own form, or mental or emotional reactions, or your own usefulness.

In Virgo, Hercules became conscious, not of soul and body placed in juxtaposition to each other, but of the fact that latent within himself was the infinite Christ; that the personality, the form side, was nurturing a beautiful hidden something, and his eyes were opened.

In Libra he went through a difficult stage of achieving equilibrium, a very abstruse sign in many ways because the man is neither the soul nor the body. Libra is the balancing on the physical plane of the pairs of opposites. He has balanced them so much that he does not feel that he is getting anywhere.

In Scorpio, on the astral plane, he takes up again the work begun in Taurus, completes it and clears away the great mire, the great illusion and stands free with the goal clear in front of him.

Gemini is the opposite of Sagittarius; Gemini duality; Sagittarius unity, the one-pointed going forward, the unified personality, conscious of the soul, determined to enter the sign Capricorn where the great transition is made out of the fourth into the fifth or spiritual kingdom.

Sagittarius is the archer on the white horse, sometimes pictured as the centaur with the bow and arrows. In these two modes of picturing – the centaur half human and half animal, the archer on the white horse, half human and half divine – you have the whole story. A white horse is always the symbol of divinity. Christ came forth riding on a white horse. There you have Sagittarius in the *Book of Revelation.* It is a double sign, and whenever you have a double sign you have a problem.

In Sagittarius, just as in Scorpio Hercules took up and completed the work started in Taurus, he took up and completed the work started in Aries. In Aries he was dealing with thought at its source. In this sign he demonstrates complete control of thought and speech.

Sagittarius has sometimes been called "the sign of the effect of Scorpio". The moment we have freed ourselves from illusion, that moment we enter into Sagittarius and we see the goal. We have never really seen it before, because between us and the goal there is always to be found that cloud of thought forms that prevents us from seeing it.

We talk about spiritual love, devotion to the Christ, devotion to the elder brothers of the race, to the soul; and as we are occupied with these thoughts we build clouds of thought forms because we are thinking, and as we think we build. Therefore we have built around ourselves such a cloud of thought forms about our aspirations, that we do not see the goal. I am not cutting away the ground under your feet, *but stop thinking so much about what to do and learn more simply "to be."*

Silence

Sagittarius is the sign preparatory to Capricorn and it is called in some ancient books "the sign of silence". In ancient mysteries the newly admitted brother had to sit in silence, he was not allowed to walk or speak; he had to be, to work and to watch, because one cannot enter the fifth kingdom in nature, the spiritual kingdom, or climb the mountain of Capricorn, until there has been restraint of speech and control of thought. *That is the lesson of Sagittarius: restraint of speech through control of thought.* That will keep us busy, because after you have given up using the ordinary forms of speech, such as gossip, then you have to learn restraint of speech about things spiritual. You have to learn what *not* to say about the life of the soul, very copious talking about things for which people may not as yet be ready.

Right use of thought, restraint of speech, and consequent harmlessness on the physical plane, result in liberation; for we are held in the human unit, we are imprisoned to the planet not by some outside force that holds us there; but by what we ourselves have said and done. The moment we no longer set up wrong relations with people by the things we say that should not have been said, the moment we stop thinking things about people that we should not think, little by little those ties that hold us to planetary existence are severed, we are freed and we climb the mountain like the goat in Capricorn.

It has been asked: "Must we never make karma for ourselves or do anything that would tie us to any human being, because as long as we tie ourselves to any human being, we have got to go on reincarnating?" Well, I am going to tie myself to humanity by service, by love, by disinterested thought. That means something. But I am not going to tie myself by critical thought, self-pitying thoughts, by gossip, by words that I should not say. I am not going to have for my motive my own liberation.

A caution: don't be good, don't be harmless, don't serve merely in order to get away from it all, which is what a lot of people do. Stay with humanity as Christ does, or like that great Life whom we are told will stay in His appointed place until the last pilgrim has found his way home.

Two Gates, Three Constellations

Sagittarius is the little gate to Capricorn. There are two cosmic gates: Cancer, the gate into incarnation; Capricorn, the gate into the spiritual kingdom. Prior to Capricorn is Sagittarius, spoken of as "a lesser gate". I like to think of it as the little gate at the foot of the hill through which we pass before climbing the mountain and in passing through that little gate, we demonstrate our ability to rightly use the arrows of thought. That is the great test.

There are two birds to be seen in the heavens close to Sagittarius. One, Aquila, the eagle flying straight into the face of the sun, the bird out of time and space, the symbol of immortality, the symbol of that secret hidden thing that lies back of our souls even; for we are told that matter or form is the vehicle for the manifestation of soul, and soul on a higher turn of the spiral is the vehicle for the manifestation of spirit, and these three are a trinity unified by life that pervades them all.

The other constellation is Cygnus, symbol of soul. Sagittarius, the aspirant, looking to the left and to the right: to the right seeing Aquila and saying to himself, "I am spirit flying straight for my home"; looking the other side and seeing Cygnus, the swan, with its four stars in the form of a cross and saying, "I am the soul crucified in matter from which I shall release myself."

Remember, the day is coming when we shall talk about the soul as we now talk about the personality, as something from which we have eventually to be released. That is the problem, if I may use that word, of the man who has taken the third initiation, to release himself from soul.

Will you take those three constellations as your symbol: Cygnus, Aquila and Sagittarius? Aquila, the eagle in the U.S. standard; the arrows of Sagittarius. And have you ever thought that wherever you go you see the cross of Cygnus, the Red Cross? That is what the United States stands for. You have it right in the heavens.

Sagittarius is the ninth sign. Think about this sequence of thought. In Virgo, the sixth sign, we have the indication of life; in Sagittarius, the ninth sign, the completion of the prenatal period before the birth of the Christ in Capricorn in December. It is amazing how your correspondences, your analogies work out. That is why we are told to study the human being. It is through the symbolism of the human being that we arrive at understanding of the great Life which includes us all in its existence.

LABOUR IX

The Chrysalis Symbol

Sagittarius, curiously enough, has been ca
stage; the man is neither one thing nor the othe.. _
you have the strange triplicity of the caterpillar, the chrysa...
and the butterfly. The caterpillar, we are told, reincarnates five
times; it sloughs its skin five times, five is the number of man.
Then there comes that curious happening in the life of the caterpillar where there is a complete change, and from a thing crawl-
ing about prompted by desire, eating all the time, there comes
the stage of the chrysalis. What goes on in that chrysalis stage
is a most mysterious happening. We are told that inside the hard
shell of chrysalis which the caterpillar has constructed, there is
nothing but a fluid. Every single thing has broken down and in
that fluid are what are called three centres of life, and because
of the interplay between those three focal points of energy, a
change goes on, a rebuilding, until there emerges out of the period of silence, a wonderful butterfly. It is almost as though in
the chrysalis there were three aspects of divinity symbolised
and working to a pattern, the Christ pattern.

Consider what goes on in the life of the individual aspirant
in Sagittarius. There has been a complete breaking down of
everything in Scorpio; everything has been reduced to fluid; for
Scorpio is an astral sign and water is the symbol. In the life of
the aspirant of today, I need not enlarge upon it, there has been
a complete breaking down of everything. As one person said to
me, there is nothing left to live for, there is nothing interesting
enough to pull one through existence. Why? Because you are
an aspirant, a disciple; it is the best indication you can have of
your status on the ladder of evolution. Everything has broken
down and you know it. But the three aspects of divinity are still
there in the fluid; and they will work and the pattern is there.
The chrysalis stage is Sagittarius. It is interesting to carry the
sequence of thought or achievement from Scorpio into the
power and success developed in Sagittarius, for it is a sign of
power.

The true Sagittarian is a very potent person; potent because is the sign of silence; potent because it is the sign of one-pointedness and the goal is seen for the first time clearly; potent because it is the period immediately preceding the birth of the Christ.

The Spirit of Truth

Sagittarius, we are told, is the spirit of truth; *it is the sum of all Truth growing out of individual revelation.*

Now the usual happening when there is an individual revelation is sectarianism; an illustration of Sagittarius misused. I had a revelation; God has revealed this, that and the other to me. I immediately impose upon my fellow men my personal interpretation of truth. I see no truth but my truth. I am an aspirant, but all aspirants must interpret truth as I see it; if not, they are not aspirants. You must believe in reincarnation because it is the truth; you must believe in the Masters of Wisdom because they exist; you must believe this, that and the other.

One-pointed, yes. But a little bit of the truth. Just so much of the truth as your poor little brain can grasp, and yet such a tremendous revelation to you that you think it is all of the truth.

In Sagittarius, the first of the great universal signs, we see truth as the whole when we are using arrows of thought rightly. I will say, this is for me, my formulation of the truth, because it helps me to live. Other groups use other terminologies and only as I can grasp my brother's way of looking at the truth is it possible for me to have the vision.

All the various truths form one Truth; that is what is realised in Sagittarius, and you cannot go through the gate at the foot of the mountain until you have seen where your little bit of truth forms part of the group mosaic. That is all.

The Spirit of Right

Sagittarius has been called the sign of the spirit of right, growing out of the contentions of the previous eight signs. When I am really functioning in Sagittarius, I will have learned to discriminate between right and wrong. I will know what is right for myself, but I will also have learned this lesson: that *my* right may be my brother's wrong, and my brother's wrong may be my right; that it is impossible for me to say what is right for you because we all have a different equipment, different heredity, different tradition and background, different racial tendencies. We are all so diverse, and carrying that thought on, we all come along different rays. We have different egoic rays and different personality rays, and the more you know about these things the less you can talk about them.

I know what is right for me and I will endeavour to live by my right, my idea of right. I do not know what is right for you, but I will give you the credit for doing the best you know. If we could assume that attitude towards each other, the spirit of harmlessness, control of thought and restraint of speech would emerge in the world and we would escape from our world problems. The world will never be put right by fighting, but by right thought, and it will be a soul process. Someone has said that in Scorpio we have conviction of sin; in Sagittarius we have conviction of right.

Three Gifts

We are told in some books on astrology that there are three signs of beneficent outpouring in the zodiac. One is Aries from which there is pouring out upon us the gift of existence. A quotation from a Hindu scripture tells us that there are three things which by the grace of God we have: the gift of being a human being, the longing for liberation, and coming under the guidance of a perfect sage, in your own heart.

The gift of existence in Aries is the wonder of being a human being. If you can think of yourself as a mineral, from such limitations you will arrive at the wonder of being, because it means freedom from the standpoint of the mineral. Complete freedom.

In Leo, the gift of opportunity. I am an individual. I shall use life for myself, if I am a little Leo; or I shall use the opportunity to open the gates for other people.

In Sagittarius, the gift of power. Do you feel able to have power? One definition of an occultist is a human being who works in the world of powers and forces. I do not know anyone who can safely be trusted to wield power. Why? Because Sagittarius has not done its work. Restraint of speech has not yet been learned. Control of thought has not been mastered, and the soul is not potent enough. When we love enough we may have power. When we love enough and are harmless enough then the gates of heaven and hell will be put into our hands, but not before.

Let us begin to love, not sentimentally, but through beginning really to understand human beings, to identify ourselves with them and love them. You can know what a human being is, with all his faults, and you can love him; not from a superior standpoint of saying "poor thing, some day he will be where I am", but from the standpoint of saying, "I have been just like that", or "I am just like that".

The gift of existence, the gift of opportunity, and the gift of power; the three great gifts of the zodiac.

Three Constellations

There are three constellations connected with this sign, the three most beautiful.

Lyra, the seven-stringed harp. The aspirant learns to play upon the harp and he makes music with his life.

Ara, the altar, because the aspirant places all upon the altar; not in the spirit of sad renunciation, bracing himself to be perfectly miserable, but in the spirit of "there is nothing else to do.

I am detaching myself from these things in order that I may more perfectly and fully serve".

Draco, the serpent. We met the hydra, the serpent, in Gemini; now we meet Draco, the serpent of wisdom.

Music in the life of harmony, sacrifices in the personality reactions and desires, and wisdom.

And hovering over two other constellations: Aquila, spirit; and Cygnus, the soul.

Do you see why I am so thrilled over Sagittarius? It is such a beautiful sign and there is so much to say about it. I have omitted so much.

Details of the Story

We read that the marshes of Acadia were filled with man-eating birds, pictured in ancient books as ferocious storks, the birds of Stymphalus. They were three in number; three major birds, but there were many small ones. They were wasting the land, but they could not be seen; they were hidden in the brush, in the undergrowth, doing damage, but they could not be located.

As usual, Hercules rushes to the land of Acadia and determines to rid the land of these man-eating birds. We are told he was very clever in the way he did it. He had freed himself from illusion and Athena had given him some cymbals which he clashed so loudly that the birds arose out of the marsh into the air and tried to fly away; then he mounted on his winged horse and shot them with his arrows. It is a wonderful story.

Marshes are a symbol of the mind plus emotion, Hercules discovers that although he may be an aspirant and he may have triumphed in Scorpio, he still possesses an emotional nature, and he finds that the birds of Stymphalus, especially three of them, are of a man-eating kind and that he must do something about it.

Picture his reaction, the conqueror discovering that he is a devastating force; that by his words and thoughts he is doing harm. Remember this, the further on you go along the path of return, and the more you function as a spiritual entity, the more potent you become and the more harm you can do. You are forceful, you are wielding power, you are probably the centre of your group. If you are an aspirant, if you are a disciple, the thought and speech activity is your main enterprise. You weigh your thoughts because there is potency back of your thought, and when you think wrongly the harm you do is much more potent than the harm that a less evolved person does.

We must get the birds out of the marshes and into the clear air where we can see them and conquer them.

The birds that did the most harm were three in number. In one book they are enumerated: cruel gossip; talk of the self, selfish talk; and casting of pearls before swine. What does that mean?

It has been said that gossip is "spiritual murder". Do I need to discuss cruel gossip, how lives have been wrecked by it? There is an unbroken law, if you gossip you will be gossiped about. We get what we give. If you give service you will get service; kindness, kindness; love, love. If humanity is mistreating you, search yourself and find out where you are at fault. An ancient scripture says, to him who is harmless all enmity ceases. I know that when I achieve harmlessness in thought, word and deed, then I will have no problems. The fact that we have problems presupposes our harmfulness.

Talking about oneself, we are always occupied with our own problems, our own affairs. Casting pearls before swine: talking about the occult troubles for which the hearers are not ready. If you are a disciple you will know to what I refer.

The problem is clear: I am a Sagittarian and so are you. We are living with the emblem of Sagittarius in front of us all the time. We are trying to bring harmony into our lives, trying to lead the "altar" life, seeking to contact the serpent of wisdom. Begin with thought and speech, and begin today.

LABOUR X.

THE SLAYING OF CERBERUS, GUARDIAN OF HADES
(Capricorn, December 22nd-January 20th)

The Myth

"The light of life must now shine forth within a world of dark," the great Presiding One declared. The Teacher understood.

"The son of man who is also the son of God must pass through Gate the tenth", he said. "Within this very hour Hercules shall venture forth."

When Hercules stood face to face with him who was his guide, the latter spoke:

"A thousand dangers you have braved, O Hercules," the Teacher said, "and much has been achieved. Wisdom and strength are yours. Will you make use of them to rescue one in agony, a prey to vast and unremitting suffering?"

The Teacher gently touched the forehead of Hercules. Before the latter's inner eye a vision rose. A man lay prone upon a rock, and groaned as if his heart would break. His hands and legs were shackled; the massive chains that bound him were tied to iron rings. A vulture, fierce and bold, kept pecking at the prostrate victim's liver; in consequence, a trickling stream of blood flowed from his side. The man uplifted his manacled hands and cried out for help; but his words echoed vainly in the desolation, and were swallowed by the wind. The vision faded. Hercules stood, as before, at the side of his guide.

"The shackled one whom you have seen is called Prometheus," the Teacher said. "For ages has he suffered thus, and yet he cannot die, being immortal. From heaven he stole the fire; for this he has been punished. The place of his abode is known as Hell, the domain of Hades. Unto Prometheus, O Hercules, you are asked to be a saviour. Go down into the depths, and there upon the outer planes release him from his suffering."

Having heard and understood, the son of man who was also a son of God, embarked upon this quest, and passed through Gate the tenth.

Downward, ever downward, did he travel into the binding worlds of form. The atmosphere grew stifling, the darkness steadily more intense. And yet his will was firm. This steep descent continued long and long. Alone, yet not all alone, he wandered on, for when he sought within he heard the silvery voice of the wisdom-goddess, Athena, and the strengthening words of Hermes.

At length he came to that dark, envenomed river called the Styx, a river that the souls of the deceased must cross. An obolus or penny had to be paid to Charon, the ferryman, that he might take them to the other side. The sombre visitor from earth affrighted Charon, and forgetting the fee, he ferried the stranger across.

Hercules at last had entered Hades, a dim and misty region where the shades, or better said, the shells of those departed flitted by.

When Hercules perceived Medusa, her hair entwined with hissing snakes, he seized his sword, and thrust at her, but struck naught save empty air.

Through labyrinthine paths he threaded his way until he came to the court of the king who ruled the underworld, Hades. The latter, grim and stern, with threatening mien, sat stiffly on his jet black throne as Hercules approached.

"What seek you, a living mortal, in my realms?" Hades demanded. Hercules said, "I seek to free Prometheus."

"The path is guarded by the monster Cerberus, a dog with three great heads, each of which has serpents coiled about it," Hades replied. "If you can conquer him with your bare hands, a feat no one has yet performed, you may unbind the suffering Prometheus."

Satisfied with this response, Hercules proceeded. Soon he saw the triple-headed dog, and heard its piercing bark. Snarling, it sprang upon him. Grasping the primary throat of Cerberus, Hercules held it in his vice-like grip. Goaded to frenzied fury, the monster thrashed about. At length, its strength subsiding, Hercules mastered it.

This done, Hercules went on, and found Prometheus. Upon a slab of stone he lay, in agonising pain. Quickly Hercules then broke the chains, and set the sufferer free.

Retracing his steps, Hercules returned as he had come. When once again he reached the world of living things, he found his Teacher there.

"The light now shines within the world of dark." the Teacher said. "The labour is achieved. Rest now, my son."

Francis Merchant.

Prologue

The sign of Capricorn, says the Tibetan, is one of the most difficult signs about which to write and is the most mysterious of all the twelve. So we have found it. Even the symbol of the sign has never been correctly drawn, we are told, because its correct delineation would produce an inflow of force that would be undesirable; also this symbol is sometimes called the "signature of God".

At the foot of the mountain the goat, the materialist, seeks for nourishment in arid places. The scapegoat on the way up finds the flowers of attained desire, each with its own thorn of satiety and disillusionment. At the top of the mountain the sacred goat sees the vision and the initiate appears. In other

writings the symbols are the goat, the crocodile and the unicorn.

One myth puts the emphasis on the descent into hell to free
humanity (in the figure of the tortured Prometheus). Another
deals more with Cerberus, some slaying him, others bringing
him up to earth. We submit these variations for the reader's consideration of their spiritual significance.

One remembers that, according to the Creed the Christed
Jesus "descended into hell". Why? Surely because his all inclusive love covered the so-called "lost souls", since we are told
that the Christ broods over humanity until the last "little one"
shall have come home.

And who are we to interpret the "signature of God"? With
humility we submit these points for pondering. We are told that
it is on his knees that the Capricornian offers heart and life to
the soul and only then, when self-initiated, can he be trusted
with the secrets of life and the higher powers.

Interpretations of the Labour in Capricorn

There are two gates of dominant importance: Cancer, into
what we erroneously call life, and Capricorn, the gate into the
spiritual kingdom. Capricorn, the gate through which we finally
pass when we no longer identify ourselves with the form side
of existence but become identified with the spirit. This is what
it means to be initiate.

An initiate is a person who is no longer placing his consciousness in his mind, or desires, or physical body. He can use
these if he chooses; and he does, to help all humanity, but that
is not where his consciousness is focused. He is focused in
what we call the soul, which is that aspect of ourselves which
is free from form. It is in soul consciousness that we eventually
function in Capricorn, know ourselves to be initiates and enter
upon two great universal signs of service to humanity. For it is
interesting that, in Aquarius, we are dealing symbolically with

animals in bulk, since in that sign Hercules has the
ing out the Augean stables, his first work as a wo
But in Pisces he captures, not the bull, but all of the oxen, carrying into our consciousness the idea of the universality of
world work, of group consciousness, of universal consciousness
and of universal service.

If you were born in the sign Capricorn, please do not get
the idea that you are an initiate. We should lay emphasis on a
sense of proportion and the status of evolution. Aspirants either
suffer from an inferiority complex that makes them feel it is not
possible to do anything, or they have an exaggerated idea of
their importance; they have a touch of soul consciousness, but
only a tiny touch, which they think is the whole thing and they
become inflated. This shows no sense of proportion.

This sign symbolises the third initiation, the first of the
major initiations. In Matthew 17 we read that Christ took three
disciples, Peter, James and John, up into a high mountain and
was transfigured before them. They fell on their faces and Peter
said, "Let us build three huts". In Hindu philosophy this is
called "initiation of the man who builds his hut." Peter, a rock
or foundation, is the symbol of the physical body. James, the
deceiver, symbolises the emotional nature, the source of all
glamour. John symbolises the mind, the name meaning, "The
Lord has Spoken." There you have the symbolism of three aspects of the personality, on their faces before the glorified
Christ, in Capricorn at his transfiguration.

Meanings of the Sign

This is the sign of the goat; it is a superhuman sign, a universal and impersonal sign. All the labours of Hercules hereto-
fore have been concerned with his own liberation. Now we
enter upon three signs that have no relation to his personal
achievements. He is free. He is an initiate, a world disciple.
He has passed round and round the zodiac, learned all the lessons of the signs and climbed the mountain of initiation; he

has undergone transfiguration; he is perfectly free and so can work universally on labours that have no relation to himself whatsoever. He works as a superhuman being in a human body. The great stages of development upon the path of expansion, which we call initiations, are recorded in the brain and *will not be told to you by someone else*. I never met a true initiate who was willing to admit that he was one, never. The hallmark of the initiate is silence. Capricorn is a sad sign, it is the sign of intense suffering and loneliness, for these also are marks of the initiate.

Impersonality is based upon a fundamental personality achievement. You must have been tremendously attached before you can know the meaning of impersonality. That is a paradox, but there is no achievement in being impersonal if there is no temptation to be personal. The impersonality we must develop is an expansion of the personal love we have for an individual, our family, our circle of friends, into exactly the same attitude for humanity, but it has nothing to do with sentimentality. We can love all mankind because we know the meaning of personal love, and we must give the same love to everybody that we have given to the individuals close to us. Impersonality is not shutting yourself off, putting up walls; it is loving everyone because we are able to see people as they truly are with their faults, their failings, their achievements, everything that goes to make them what they are and, seeing them clear-eyed, to love them just the same. In the Rules of the Road it is written: "Each sees and knows the villainy of each. And yet there is, with that great revelation, no turning back, no spurning of each other". That is the condition to be attained in Capricorn. That which we have to develop does not come by hardening the heart, nor by tremendous detachment, nor by climbing a pedestal.

The world disciple does not only do what Hercules did, go down into hell to conquer Cerberus, but he works among men all the time, interested in his fellow man. He is impersonal. I wonder if this impersonality does not refer to ourselves rather than to the other persons. We talk, about being impersonal in our dealing. If we were quite impersonal in dealing with ourselves, our reactions to our fellowmen would be just right.

Constellations

There are three constellations connected with the sign Capricorn. One is called *Sagitta,* the arrow. It has no connection with the sign Sagittarius. In that sign we had the bowman with the arrow whereby the achieving aspirant pierced the personality. Here you have the arrow that comes from a cosmic source, piercing the heart of the son of God, called the Christ, the nearest to us of the great world saviours, "a man of sorrows and acquainted with grief". He was pierced by the arrow Sagitta, the cosmic arrow.

The Hebrew name for this arrow means "the desolate one", and the path that every disciple treads is necessarily a lonely one. The path of the initiate is more lonely still. The path of a world saviour is the most lonely of all. I think that this condition is going to be alleviated. Down the ages we have had these tremendous comings out, one here, one there. Have you ever considered their loneliness? They had none who understood. Perhaps they were canonised hundreds of years after they died. But now there are so many aspirants, so many upon the path of discipleship, that perhaps the group consciousness which is beginning to demonstrate in world affairs will result in a group loneliness rather than in individual loneliness.

Aquila, the eagle, is regarded as being as closely related to Capricorn as to Sagittarius. You have the bird of light (symbol of the highest aspect of man) manifesting as the soul (the second aspect) which has achieved.

In *Delphinus* you have a very interesting constellation that holds in it an amazing piece of symbolism. It is pictured in an ancient zodiac as a fish full of life leaping out of the water into the air and playing. That is the symbol of the son of God who, working under the law, takes form and lives in the water and in the air; and since he is no longer held by the physical law he can play with the forces of nature. We are beginning to learn about these forces, but it will be some time yet before Delphinus, the dolphin, will have much personal significance for us.

The Climbing of the Mountain

Capricorn tells the story of the climbing of the mountain and of the descent into hell. There are three great ascensions of every soul. Masonry down the ages has been a custodian of this tradition. First there is the raising of matter into heaven. We find that in Virgo. Then there is the raising up of the psychic nature from below the diaphragm. You are no longer emotional and self-centred, living in the solar plexus, but are focused in the heart and are conscious of the group; your feelings and desires are related to the group.

You no longer live in the animal nature, interested in creation on the physical plane, but you become a spiritual creature working in mental matter. You are no longer held by form, but have so dealt with it that you have raised it to the head consciousness and from the head you control your throat, your heart, your solar plexus and every part of your body. You do this not by centering on them, not by thinking about them, but by living as a conscious son of God seated on "the throne between the eyebrows", the ajna centre (or pituitary gland) as the Hindus name it. That is the second great ascension.

The final ascension is that which marks the emancipation of the initiate of very high degree who becomes consciously a world saviour. But it is the second initiation, the raising up of the lower psychic nature, on which we have to work so that every desire, mood and every emotion is lifted up into "heaven".

Preparation for the Descent into Hades

There were three things that Hercules had to do before starting down into hell. The order in which they came is interesting.

First he had to purify himself. Hercules, the son of God who had triumphed, been transfigured, was going down into hell to work and the word came to purify himself. He thought he was so pure. How he underwent the process of purification we are not told, but I have the idea that he had to demonstrate freedom from irritability and selfishness in that uninteresting circle where he was living as a human being. It is a rule in occultism that, on the ladder of initiation, if you cannot live purely in your own home circle you are of no use in heaven or hell. What do I mean by "pure"? We use the word largely in its physical sense but "pure" really is freedom from the limitations of matter. If I am in any way imprisoned even by my mind, which is a form of subtle matter, I am not pure. If I have any selfish emotions, I am not pure. Hercules had to purify himself.

Then we read that he had to be initiated into the mysteries. As far as I can understand it (and I may be wrong) this means that you go through your own personal hell before you can go through the universal hell. You have a terrible time in your own life and you are initiated as you undergo your own hell. You learn the nature of the universal by individual experience; only that is realisation. You cannot learn by hearsay.

As has happened before in the myths, Hercules then had to pause and perform an act of service before he could advance upon Cerberus. He saw two people bound and being attacked by cattle. He had to deliver them before he could meet his own problem. Always for the initiate service comes first; the letting go of what he has set himself to do if there is need to help. That is the story of the initiate always, because it is based on group consciousness.

The Symbol of Cerberus

The three-headed dog Cerberus with a terrific bark, with snakes growing out all over his body and with snakes for a tail, was the guardian of Hades. The three heads symbolise sensation, desire and good intentions. It is love of sensation that drives humanity hither and thither to satisfy hunger in the economic world or to satisfy desire for happiness in the world of pleasure. The violent impacts of sensation are sought to keep the mind occupied. The central head was grasped by Hercules first because it was the most important, since desire underlies all sensations; it is what desire seeks to express and so gain satisfaction in the outer world. The third head is good intentions, not carried out. So you have desire in the centre, on one side you have sensation typifying all impacts, and on the other side the third head of good intentions not thought through, never performed, of which it has long been said: "Hell is paved with good intentions".

The tail made of serpents typifies all illusions that impede the progress of spiritual life; the materiality that holds us down; the lower psychic nature that causes such destruction; fear along every possible line; the fear of failure which holds so many back from activity and breeds only inertia, the great fault, we are told, of aspirants and disciples.

Hercules grasped Cerberus by the central head and conquered him, because all sun gods are occupied with the problems of humanity and because desolate they go down into hell alone to save humanity; hence all sun gods are born in the sign of Capricorn.

Lecture by A.A.B., condensed and edited.

Epilogue

The great swing in Capricorn is epitomised by the keywords. Upon the ordinary wheel these are, "And the word said: let ambition rule and let the door stand wide." This is the key to the evolutionary urge and the secret of rebirth. (The Tibetan). When a true sense of reality supersedes both earthly and spiritual ambition the man can say with truth, "lost am I in light supernal, yet on that light I turn my back." So goes the world disciple, initiate in Capricorn, on his way to serve humanity in

Aquarius. In that sign he cleans the Augean stables (of the karma of all past ignorance and error, the Dweller on the Threshold) and so becomes in Pisces a world saviour. One remembers that the last act of the Christ on his way to Gethsemane and Calvary was to wash the feet of his disciples.

It has been said: "Christianity has not failed: it has never been tried." Are we now, after two thousand years, really beginning to try, individually and in group formation? This is the work that makes it possible for the Christ to reappear and also which prepares humanity to recognise him and to be able to endure the quality of the emanations that attend his coming.

Amplification of *Esoteric Astrology,* pp. 153-174.

Let every man remember that the destiny of mankind is incomparable and that it depends greatly on his will to collaborate in the transcendent task. Let him remember that the law is, and always has been, to struggle; and that the fight has lost nothing of its violence by being transposed from the material onto the spiritual plane. Let him remember that his own dignity, his nobility as a human being, must emerge from his efforts to liberate himself from his bondage and to obey his deeper aspirations. And let him above all never forget that the divine spark is in him, in him alone, and that he is free to disregard it, to kill it, or to come closer to God by showing his eagerness to work with Him, and for Him.

Le Comte du Noüy.

LABOUR XI.

CLEANSING THE AUGEAN STABLES
(Aquarius, January 21st-February 19th)

The Myth

Within the Place of Peace the Great Presiding One poured forth the radiance of his exalted thought. The Teacher drew nigh.

"The single flame must light the other forty-nine," the Great Presiding One affirmed.

"So be it," the Teacher answered. "Having lit his own lamp Hercules now must bring the Light to others." Not long thereafter, the Teacher summoned Hercules.

"Eleven times the wheel has turned, and now you stand before another Gate. For long you have pursued the light which flickered first uncertainly, then waxed to a steady beacon, and now shines for you like a blazing sun. Turn now your back upon the brightness; reverse your steps; go back to those for whom the light is but a transient point, and help them make it grow. Direct your steps to Augeas whose kingdom must be cleansed of ancient evil. I have spoken"

Forth went Hercules through Gate the eleventh in search of Augeas the king.

When Hercules approached the realm where Augeas was the ruler, a horrid stench that made him faint and weak assailed his nostrils. For years, he learned, King Augeas had never cleared away the dung his cattle left within the royal stables. Then, too, the pastures were so amply dunged, no crops could grow. In consequence, a blighting pestilence was sweeping through the land, wreaking havoc with human lives.

To the palace then went Hercules and sought out Augeas. Informed that Hercules would cleanse the stenchy stables, Augeas displayed distrust and disbelief.

"You say that you will do this mighty task without reward?" the King declared suspiciously. "I have no faith in those who make such boasts. Some cunning plan you have contrived, O Hercules, to take my throne from me. Of men who seek to serve the world without a recompense, I have not heard. At this point, though, I'd welcome any fool who sought to help. But a bargain must be struck, lest I be chided as a foolish king. If you, within a single day, shall do what you have promised, one-tenth of my great flock of cattle shall be yours; but if you fail, your life and fortune will be in my hands. Of course, I do not think you can fulfil your boast, but try you may."

Hercules then left the King. He wandered through the blighted place, and saw a cart go by piled high with dead, the victims of the pestilence.

Two rivers, he observed, the Alpheus and the Peneus, flowed quietly nearby. Standing on the banks of one, the answer to his problem flashed upon his mind.

With might and main he laboured. By great exertions he succeeded in diverting both these streams from courses they had followed for decades. The Alpheus and the Peneus were made to pour their waters through the dung-filled stables of King Augeas. The rushing torrents swept away the long-accumulated filth. The realm was purged of all its fetid murk. Within a single day the task impossible had been performed.

When Hercules, quite satisfied with this result, returned to Augeas, the latter scowled.

"You have succeeded by a trick," King Augeas cried out in rage. "The rivers did the work, not you. It was a ruse to take from me my cattle, a plot against my throne. Rewards you shall not have. Go, get you hence ere I cut down your stature by a head."

The angry King thus banished Hercules, and bade him nevermore set foot within his realm on penalty of sudden death.

Having performed the task assigned, the son of man who also was the Son of God went back to him from whom he came.

"A server of the world you have become," the Teacher said when Hercules drew nigh. "You have gone on by going back; you have come to the House of Light by yet another path; you have spent your light that the light of others might shine. The jewel that the eleventh labour gives is yours forever more."

Francis Merchant.

The Energies of Aquarius
Lecture by A.A.B. 1937

There is a phrase in the New Testament, "The end of the world". It is just beginning to dawn upon many of us that what was really meant was that the sign Pisces, in which Christ, the Great World Saviour; came, would end at a particular date, and we are right in that time now. We are not facing a judgment day in which the sheep and goats will be divided and some go to heaven and others go to hell. Many ridiculous interpretations have been put upon the symbolism of the Bible.

It has been thought that the sheep went to heaven and the goats went to hell. It is the other way round. The goat in Capricorn is the initiate and from a certain esoteric angle the goats do go to heaven because they function in the spiritual kingdom which is heaven; the sheep remain on earth (which after all is the only hell one can possibly predicate) until they are no longer sheep, until they learn to have individual thought, become goats, climb the mountain and exchange the position of follower to that of independent seekers.

Entrance into heaven is entrance into the Aquarian age, begun during the last two hundred years. We are told that about the year two thousand our pole star and another star (Vega) in the heavens will be in conjunction with each other and the

Aquarian age will be fully with us, but only fully with us in the sense that we shall be entering it and Piscean forces will be receding rapidly. All that transpires in physical plane expression is due to subjective forces.

A school of thought exists which traces all the mysteries, all the teachings that we are now calling the Ageless Wisdom, to a form of animal worship and temple mysteries of a sordid and sexual kind. I shall not go into details, but I want to tell you what I think is of vital interest for us to grasp, because it is something in the Aquarian age which will be emerging in greater fullness right along. It is one thing to be subjected to blind force, it is another to have an intelligent outlook upon what is happening and to understand and look for certain occurrences. Perhaps for the first time in the history of our race there is a sufficient number of intelligent men and women to anticipate happenings with an understanding based on what has transpired in the past, so enabling them to predicate what will happen in the future.

What caused the worship of the bull in Taurus? Not the bestial nature of humanity that took the bull as a symbol of the animal nature and deified it, which is what the average human being who investigates the mysteries says. It is because there were subjective forces playing upon our planet as our sun passed through the sign Taurus. The lesson for man is that under the symbol of the bull he had to wrestle with the animal in himself.

Then our sun passed into Aries, the Ram, and we had the sacrifice of the lamb, showing that the sacrifice of the animal nature was beginning to succeed the concept of wrestling with the animal nature.

Then the sun passed into Pisces, the fishes. The forces that played upon our planet at that time brought into the consciousness of man his essential duality and the link between the two parts of himself, two fishes linked by a band. This consciousness, on a large scale, began to make its impact upon the human being, i.e. that he is soul and body. Christ came in Pisces to demonstrate to us perfectly what would be our ultimate achievement when we had linked those two together, the fish, the symbol of the second person, the fish Avatar, and the fish swimming in matter, the symbol of the human being in incarnation. There you have the story.

Having traced that wonderful, idealistic, evolutionary teaching down the last five to six thousand years as the result of subjective forces playing upon humanity, we are now passing into the sign Aquarius where, through symbolism of water and purification, we shall learn how to be the soul and not the human being. That is what is going to happen in Aquarius.

At the end of the Aquarian age, approximately two thousand five hundred years hence, can you picture what humanity will be like? The animal nature, the emotional nature and the mentality will be secondary, and the soul, the consciousness aspect, that universal urge in each of us that puts us en rapport with God, will have surged to the front. Putting it another way, we shall have left behind the human kingdom and, though we may be inhabiting bodies, our consciousness will be focused in the fifth kingdom of nature, the spiritual kingdom. That is the prophecy, the thing that lies ahead for humanity in two thousand five hundred years' time.

The opposite sign to Aquarius is Leo, the sign of the individual, the man who has found himself as a human being. He stood upon his own feet; he was the centre of his universe; the stars revolved around him, everything happened in relation to himself. By that he learned certain great lessons: that it was just possible he was not as important as he thought, and that by subjecting himself to certain training he could find a larger self; and so he passed on into Scorpio, where he was tested to see how much persistence he had. The outstanding characteristic of the aspirant is endurance and the sign that calls for the utmost endurance is Scorpio. He triumphs in Scorpio. and in Sagittarius he becomes the one-pointed disciple who, having put his hand to the plough, *cannot turn back*; he may want to but he cannot turn back. He goes on, and because he goes on he climbs to the top of the mountain in Capricorn and undergoes the transfiguration.

In Aquarius the disciple becomes the serving master. We shall take up the subject of world saviours in Pisces. In Aquarius the man is a serving master. That is the keynote I want you to hold in your minds. He can be a master because he has learned to serve, and he can serve because he is a master. Those two go together.

The ruler of the first decanate of Aquarius is Saturn. Saturn gives us discipline; Saturn opens for us the door of opportunity. Saturn, through spiritual exercises and trials, strengthens our spiritual muscles and enables us to emerge out of darkness into light.

Hallmarks of the Initiate

Hercules being the initiate is pledged to do three things, which can be summed up as the outstanding characteristics of all true initiates. If they are not present in some measure the man is not an initiate.

1. *Unselfish service.* This is not the service that we render because we are told that service is a way to liberation, but service rendered because our consciousness is no longer self centred. We are no longer interested in ourselves but our consciousness being universal there is nothing for us to do but to assimilate the troubles of our fellowmen and help them. It is no effort for the true Aquarian master to do so.

2. *Group work.* This is something that we know little about as yet. The world is full of organisations and societies, brotherhoods that are happy training grounds for ambitious people. I do not mean to be unkind, but my experience with the average group is that it is a hotbed of jealousies, people trying to impress the others with the amount of their knowledge and the wonder of their self-sacrificing lives. This is not group work.

Group work is standing alone spiritually in the handling of one's own affairs with complete forgetting of one's own self and affairs in the welfare of the particular section of humanity with which we are associated. It negates ambition; it negates the progress upward in any lodge or organisation; it negates all assuming of official prerogatives. I do not think the new groups will have any officials but will work automatically because of the intuitional spiritual interplay between the minds of the units in the groups. We do not know anything about it yet.

Can you think of a group so united on spiritual levels that letters, pamphlets, books, etc., can be done away with; that the intercommunication between the minds of the members of the group is perfect? That is the Aquarian group and it is not with us yet.

3. *Self-sacrifice.* The meaning of self-sacrifice is making the self holy. That deals with the self of the group and the self of the individual; that is the work of the initiate.

From the top of the mountain in Capricorn, Hercules has to come down literally into material filth and clean the Augean stables. I want to give you an idea of his psychology. He had climbed up to the top of the mountain. He had passed all the great tests, passed from Capricorn into the spiritual kingdom and knew somewhat the significance of mystical ecstasy, and in that highly spiritual state he received word to go down and clean the stables. What an anti-climax. No great world work, but to clean stables.

The object of the test can be summed up in this way: Hercules had to aid in the cleansing of the world by the right direction of the forces of life through it. You appreciate that we are entering into the Aquarian age where materialism, as we know it, will have completely died out at the close and when the whole life will be interpreted in terms of energies. We are dealing entirely with forces. We shall probably have a new language, the symbolic language of energy itself. We shall all be practical occultists, the occultist who lives and works in a world of forces and who begins with the forces within himself. You will get a little understanding of what is meant by the wielding of forces if you watch your speech. Why do you raise your voice when emoting? Because the energy sweeping through you has an effect upon your vocal apparatus. You are dealing with energies and you are misusing energies. Watch yourself and begin to work in the world of forces within yourself.

This sign inaugurates the school of world saviours. It is almost a "John the Baptist" sign, a sign of preparation for what the next Piscean age is going to bring in.

Aquarius is depicted as a man holding an inverted vase. The man inverts the vase and out of it come two streams of water, the river of life and the river of love, and those two words, life and love, are the two worlds that embody the technique of the Aquarian age; not form, not mind, but life and love. Two words we use constantly but which, back of them, do not bear any adequate concept.

Decanates, Rulers and Constellations

Aquarius, like other signs, is divided into three decanates. We are now entering the first decanate governed by Saturn, hence our present difficulties, our political upheaval, the dividing of the world stage into great groups, with people who are national, patriotic, and those who are beginning to vision the international spirit. In the churches, in the religious field, division again, between those who are getting a picture of the universality of the love of God, and those who bow to authority and dogma.

In the field of economics a tremendous turmoil is brought about by Saturn, between those who bow to material things and those who are letting them go in order to get the better things; between those who grab possessions for themselves, those who hoard and keep, and those who let go in order to acquire what Christ calls "treasures in heaven". In almost any field of thought we find these two compelling forces because of the impact of Piscean and Aquarian energies. There are two diverse groups: those who are tied to the past and to the material aspect and those who are getting the vision and are seeing the life, the consciousness, the purpose and the plan emerging through the medium of them all.

The wonderful thing, if you study the world intuitively, if you keep apace with what is going on in this and other sections of humanity, is that you will see that, in spite of superficial disturbances and dire happenings, the spirit of man is sound and pure, is rising to the occasion and we are coming through, but don't think it will be in a week or a year! We may get better conditions, improvements here, there and everywhere. It is up to us how fast we learn the lesson of how to let go, in order that the Piscean age of materialism and of authority, possession and mentality can be superseded by the age of spirituality, of intuition, and of universal consciousness.

The second decanate of Aquarius is governed by Mercury, and out of the present time will come illumination. The illumination that came in Leo, the opposite of Aquarius, was "I am the self", the illumination we call self consciousness. Illumination coming in Aquarius is "I am That", I am group conscious. My self consciousness has dropped away, my individuality is of no importance, my personality is only a mechanism, and my consciousness is one with all that is.

In the third decanate, governed by Venus, we have the emergence of inclusive love. About two thousand years from now we may really express brotherly love. It will be, must be, a manifested fact before humanity *as a whole* can pass into Capricorn. They will enter that sign in a loving spirit. The individual aspirant cannot take initiation until he has learned to love disinterestedly, to love not only those who think as he does and act as he desires.

The lawgivers

There are two lawgivers in the Zodiac, *Regulus* and *Kefus*. In Leo we have one of the four royal stars, *Regulus* the lawgiver; the law for the individual, the law of selfishness, if you like, the law of competition, the law that sets every man against his fellowman, the law that makes him grab and grasp, the law under which we live, the law of competition.

Regulus, the law of the individual, has to give place to *Kefus,* the law of Aquarius, where we shall have a new law based on suffering, illumination and love. It would be interesting to see how far you yourself can grasp what those types of law will be, based upon the suffering of the individual that has led him to lose interest in himself. When you have suffered enough you do not care about yourself any more. You find that the only way to happiness is not to be free from suffering but to lose yourself in something outside yourself.

The Aquarian law is based on spiritual illumination, on intuitive perception and brotherly love which is identification with every form in every kingdom in nature. A tremendous future lies ahead; two thousand five hundred years will have been consummated. We are on our way.

Remember, the more rarefied the forms through which the life is acting, the more rapid the reaction. That is why we have this tremendous speed in every department of life, why we are all so strung up. We have Piscean bodies and we are trying to vibrate to the Aquarian age. *We are not Aquarians yet;* there are no true Aquarians; we are not yet equipped. For that age some of the children coming in have the earmarks, but even they are few and far between.

The Aquarian age is going to manifest over the whole world; there will be Aquarians born everywhere because there is the working out of the subjective spirit in every part of the planet. It is possible that in America, Canada, Australia, New Zealand and South Africa there will be focal points of the energy, but what will really happen is the coming into incarnation all over the world in every kingdom of nature of those human beings and other forms of life, all merging under the new Aquarian influence. A marvellous thing is taking place; let us get the world ready so that our children, and children's children, can see it all happen.

Christ sounded the note "for the time of the end" when he said. "A new commandment I give unto you, that you love one another." The eleventh commandment, eleventh sign. It is only now we are discovering what a marvellous astrologer Christ was. He knew that the cycle he inaugurated would pass away, that a new method of work would have to emerge whereby the Masters would employ a new mode of reaching humanity, but he prepared the way for his own later work.

There are three constellations in Aquarius. The Southern Fish, *Pisces Australes,* picturing in connection with Aquarius the coming world saviours. Note that here, in the culmination of Pisces, we have one fish, the avatar, not the two fishes banded together. The second constellation is *Pegasus,* the winged horse, ever the inspiring symbol of the higher mind, love, spurning the earth, at home in the air. On a lower level we are reminded of the winged feet of Mercury, ever wings of the mind, remembering also that one definition of love is "the cold, clear light of reason". The third constellation takes yet a further flight, for we have *Cygnus,* the Swan, flying in mid-heaven. The swan of eternity, flying in time and space, is the symbol of Life itself, the cleansing, purifying "living waters" of Aquarius.

Interpolated

Interpretation of the Test

Augeas, the son of Neptune, the god of the waters and the sun, kept herds of animals and for thirty years the stables had not been cleared so that the filth had accumulated. Hercules was told to do something about it; many people had attempted to clean the stables and failed; it was always beyond them.

Hercules being an initiate and having much common sense, which real initiates always have, went down from the mountain top and contemplated the problem; he studied the stables.

First he broke down the wall that surrounded the stables, then he made two great holes in its opposite sides, and turned two rivers through them. He did not try to sweep and clean, as others had, but he broke down barriers by using two rivers. Without effort on his part the stables were cleaned.

Very pleased with himself Hercules rushed off to Augeas and shouted, "I have cleaned the stables. They are perfectly clean." And we read that Augeas turned his back on him, refused to recognise what he had done, and said it was a trick.

It might be said that the emotional desire nature of that great Life in Whom we live and move and have our being, also keeps herds of animals that answer to the name of human beings!

To my mind, the word God, three little letters, is just a symbol. I do not pretend to know what it is a symbol of, but I know it stands for me as a symbol of a life that is immanent in all forms and transcendent also. I am one of the herd animals that has been kept by Augeas, and the stables in which the animals dwelt have not been cleaned for 30 years, 3 multiplied by 10, and 3 is the number of the personality and 10 is the number of completion.

What if I told you that now, in your day and mine, for the first time humanity is a co-ordinated complete unit with mind, emotional nature and physical body functioning as one, and that the stables have not been cleaned for 30 years?

What are the two things that Hercules did? He broke down the barriers. That is the first thing that has to happen in the Aquarian age. We are just beginning to do it. We are just beginning to think in broad terms, to leave off being exclusive. Emerging in the world are groups of men and women everywhere who are wrestling with themselves in order to be inclusive in their thought, because in the Aquarian age nations as we know them now will have to go; nations fighting for themselves and for what they want, nation against nation, the cultivation of patriotism which is frequently the cultivation of hatred. We have to teach people that they are human beings with certain responsibilities, yes, but we can begin to get a larger picture, develop the consciousness of humanity as a whole. As Browning says:

> "Mankind made up of all the single men
> In such a unity the picture ends."

That is going to happen in Aquarius, that is what lies ahead, that is what the United Nations, movements for international peace and other groups in religious, political and economic fields are working for; the breaking down of prejudice and learning to think in general terms, in wholes. The breaking down of barriers on a large scale has to be brought about by public opinion, and this is of slow growth and largely emotional; that is the trouble.

In the Aquarian age, especially in the second decanate, when Mercury the messenger from the soul to the brain via the mind is ruling, we will have public opinion moulded by thought and not by emotion, and we shall have the world full of thinkers. The function of those who write and think along these lines, and there are thousands everywhere in the world, is to begin to think constructively along right lines so that the foundations will be well laid for the force pouring in; we build for the future.

Inclusive consciousness does not mean humanly conscious; it is more, you must become time conscious. The time is coming in Aquarius when past, present and future will pass out altogether and you will always have the eternal present that will include every sphere and aspect of consciousness which we can call strictly human. That is the position of the humanist, as I interpret it; he takes the position "Let us be truly human" before we attempt to be superhuman. We are now only emotional, watery, fluidic creatures that are as yet unilluminated, struggling with separativeness. We are not able to be world conscious, to be en rapport with every phase of human thought. We shall be some day.

Let me ask a question. Are you able to enter intelligently, sympathetically and understandingly into the consciousness of the immediate members of your family and know why they think as they do, understanding why they act in a particular way under a particular condition? Cultivate the Aquarian spirit of leaving people free, cultivate the capacity of trust. Cut out distrust of all with whom you associate, believe in them and they will not let you down. Impute wrong motives and they will let you down and it will be your own fault. Let us be as fair as we can with the light we have. Let us cultivate the Aquarian spirit of non-separativeness, love, understanding, intelligence, free from authority, drawing out of every human being we meet the best that is in them. And if you do not draw out of them the best in them, blame yourself and not them. That is the truth. If a person misinterprets you, it is because you are not clear. Self reference is always necessary for the Aquarian, but not that self-consciousness that we find now.

When we have broken down barriers of separativeness, then we let in the two rivers, the water of life and the river of love. I cannot talk, about those two rivers because I do not know what they are. Many talk about life and love; they use words. I do not know what life is yet, and we certainly do not know what love is.

It is interesting to try to express to yourself what you understand by the river of life and the river of love which, by breaking down the walls, flow through the human family. We are entering increasingly into the age of energy, entering into the age of love. Do you appreciate that a great hole was made in walls during the war; and that since the war, life and energy have come to mean something more than they did before?

When you have done all you can to break down the walls and to express life and love, aided by your own soul whose nature is love-wisdom, do not look for recognition; you won't get it. The hard task of the pioneer in any field of thought, of any person who is endeavouring to express the new ideals, is always non-recognition and sometimes worse. You won't be praised, you won't be pitied, you will have a difficult time, but remember, you are hewing the path so that in the future, hatred and separation may die out.

I like to think of Aquarius as the "John the Baptist sign" in terms of the initiate. We are leaving Pisces in one respect and we are headed toward a Piscean era in another respect when the World Saviour will come. And as we look upon the Aquarian age as a John the Baptist sign, so we can look upon ourselves in our own fields wherever we may be. In view of the cosmic picture, doing all we can do at this particular time, we are fulfilling the function of John the Baptist and preparing the way for that extraordinary happening that is going to take place individually when the World Saviour will again emerge and humanity will learn the next great truth and step forward and up.

Alice A. Bailey.

LABOUR XII.

THE CAPTURE OF THE
RED CATTLE OF GERYON
(Pisces, February 20th-March 20th)

The Myth

Within the sacred Council Chamber, the great Presiding One revealed unto the Teacher the Will of What Must Be.

"Lost he is, and found; dead, yet vibrant with Life. The server becomes the saviour, and homeward turns."

The Teacher pondered; then he called for Hercules. "Before the last gate now you stand," the Teacher said, "One labour yet remains before the circle is complete, and liberation is attained. Proceed to that dark place called Erytheia where Great Illusion is enthroned where Geryon, the monster of three heads, three bodies and six hands, is lord and king. Unlawfully he holds a herd of dark red cattle. From Erytheia to our Sacred City must you drive this herd. Beware of Eurytion, the shepherd, and his two-headed dog, Orthrus." He paused. "One caution I can give," he added slowly. "Invoke the aid of Helius."

Through Gate the Twelfth the son of man who was also the Son of God departed. In search of Geryon he went.

Within a temple Hercules made offerings to Helius, the god of fire in the sun. For seven days he meditated, and then a favour was bestowed on him. A golden chalice fell upon the ground before his feet. He knew within himself that this bright object would enable him to cross the seas to reach the land of Erytheia.

And so it was. Within the safe protection of the golden chalice, he sailed across the tossing seas until he came to Erytheia. Upon a strand in that far country, Hercules debarked.

195

Not long thereafter he came upon the pasture land where the red-hued cattle grazed. Guarded were they by the shepherd Eurytion and the double-headed dog, Orthrus.

When Hercules approached, the dog sped forward like an arrow to its target. Upon the visitor the creature hurled itself, snarling viciously, its bared fangs fiercely snapping. With one decisive blow did Hercules lay the monster low.

Then Eurytion, fearful of the brave warrior who stood before him, supplicated that his life be spared. Hercules conceded his request. Driving the blood-red cattle before him, Hercules turned his face toward the Sacred City.

Not far had he gone when he perceived a distant cloud of dust that rapidly grew larger. Surmising that the monster Geryon had come in mad pursuit, he turned to face his foe. Soon Geryon and Hercules stood face to face. Breathing fire and flame from all three heads at once, the monster came upon him.

Geryon hurled a spear at Hercules that almost hit its mark. Stepping agilely aside, Hercules evaded the deadly shaft.

Stretching taut his bow, Hercules let fly an arrow that seemed to burn the air as he released it, and struck the monster squarely in the side. With such great impetus had it been shot that all three bodies of fierce Geryon were pierced. With a shrill, despairing groan, the monster swayed, then fell, nevermore to rise.

Toward the Sacred City, then, Hercules drove the sleek, red cattle. Difficult was the task. Again and yet again some cattle strayed, and Hercules would leave the herd in search of errant wanderers.

Across the Alps he drove his cattle, and into Italy. Wherever wrong had triumphed he dealt the powers of evil a deadly blow, and righted the balance in favour of justice. When Eryx the wrestler challenged him, Hercules cast him down so forcefully that there he stayed. Again, when the giant Alcyoneus threw a rock that weighed a ton at Hercules, the latter caught it on his club, and hurled it back to kill the one who sent it forth.

At times he lost his way, but always Hercules turned back, retraced his steps, and journeyed on. Though wearied by this most exacting labour, Hercules at last returned. The Teacher awaited his coming.

"Welcome, O Son of God who is also a son of man," he greeted the returning warrior. "The jewel of immortality is yours. By these twelve labours have you overcome the human, and put on the divine. Home have you come, no more to leave. Upon the starry firmament your name shall be inscribed, a symbol to the struggling sons of men of their immortal destiny. The human labours ended, your cosmic tasks begin."

From out the Council Chamber came a voice that said, "well done, O Son of God."

Frances Merchant.

Interpretation of the Story

There are several variations of the myth concerning the labour of Hercules in the sign Pisces. We are told that there was an island where lived a human monster called Geryon with a body of three men united. He had a herd of red cattle, guarded by a shepherd and a two-headed dog. Hercules received orders (Pisces is the sign of obedience) to bring these cattle from the island, across land and water to the sacred city.

Hercules sailed to the island in a golden cup and when he arrived there he climbed to the top of a mountain and spent the night in prayer. Then he killed the two-headed dog but he did not kill the shepherd. He also killed the owner of the red cattle. Here is the beautiful part of the story: Hercules placed all of the cattle in the golden cup, in which he had sailed over to the island, took them to the Sacred City, and offered them in sacrifice to Athena, Goddess of Wisdom. This sacred city consisted of two towns connected by a wonderful wall and a gateway called the Gateway of the Lion. After the cattle were delivered Hercules' work was over. We hear no more about him but he may have gone on to greater cosmic work.

Let us think of Hercules as a world saviour. He has had a vision of something he has to do. He sees humanity owned by a monster, a three-bodied man, the symbol of a human being with mental, emotional and physical bodies united. I think that this labour has not yet been completed; this accomplishment lies ahead. There have been other sons of men gathered out of the human family from time to time, one here one there, a group here and another there, as when the Buddha was on earth and it is said that he saved nine hundred. Now humanity, the human monster; is ready for salvation and the real work of The World Saviour can begin as a whole with the group concept underlying the work rather than individual soul saving.

The symbolism of the red cattle is plainly that of the lower desires, desire being ever an outstanding characteristic of humanity. They are guarded by a shepherd, which is the mind, the two-headed dog representing the matter aspect and the psychic nature. You see why Hercules spared the shepherd. The mind can still be the shepherd of the cattle but the two-headed dog, the psychic-emotional nature and the matter aspect, Hercules killed, which means that they were deprived of any power. The shepherd still had power and I can conceive of no time in which a human being in incarnation will not need to use the mind as the interpreter of spiritual energy.

If Jesus as a human being, en rapport with his soul, becomes a transmitter of light to the sons of men, so we can extend the concept and think of humanity as a whole with all minds held steady in the light, transmitting to lower kingdoms in nature that spiritual energy which will raise them up into heaven. That is the work of humanity. We are so occupied with our own problems that we forget the larger picture. It is to be noted again that the keeper of the cattle, the form aspect, was also killed but the shepherd and the cattle were raised up in the golden cup. Here you have the Holy Grail; and so the work was accomplished. The World Saviour had fulfilled his function; He had lifted up humanity. That is what all world saviours have done. They all did what, to a greater extent, Christ did.

We hear about the failure of Christianity. I do not see failure anywhere in the Great Plan. Perhaps slowness, but do you know how disastrous it would be if evolution were too rapid, how dangerous it would be if people were overstimulated before they were ready? All teachers know the dangers of overstimulation, the disasters that occur when a person makes certain contacts before the mechanism is sufficiently tuned up. World saviours have to work slowly, but time means nothing to them.

The term, world saviour, has until now been associated with the thought of the emergence of a great son of God out of the Father's home, called by the need of humanity to do a great work. Down the ages they have come, dwelt in physical bodies, worked through an emotional nature and have been exceedingly intelligent. They have by their lives set an example that we may follow in their steps; by their words they have sounded the note, the message that humanity needed in order to take the immediate next step forward. In their acts they have given a demonstration of service, gone about the world doing good, and their names have stayed with us down the ages. You must be a very dominant figure to remain in the minds of men for thousands of years. Most of us are forgotten in twenty.

Significant Aspect of the Sign

The sign Pisces marks a triangular place in the heavens, a symbol of reality. This sign rules the feet and hence the idea of treading the Path and attaining the goal has been the underlying spiritual revelation of the Piscean age.

Pisces is also the sign of death in various aspects. The death of the body sometimes, or it may be that an old foolishness has come to an end, an undesirable friendship will cease, devotion to some religious form of thought that has held you will now end and you will emerge and set your feet upon a new path. It is the sign of death to the personality. If we could give up the idea of the personality veils, we would be willing to let the personality go. It also means the death of a world saviour for it is the sign of crucifixion and marks the end of a zodiacal cycle.

There are three signs of salvation in the Zodiac. First, Leo, where the word goes out to the human being, "work out your own salvation". So we have in Leo the man determined to stand on his own legs, he becomes bumptious and assertive but this is necessary to salvation because only by trying out his equipment will he arrive at the point where a broader view appears. The second sign of salvation is Sagittarius, the sign of service and silence, where the assertive man, tired of talking of himself and pushing himself forward, loses sight of himself in the goal and silently serves. Then we come to the third sign Pisces, that of world saviours.

The first constellation in Pisces is that curious cluster of stars called "The Band", connecting the two fishes, one fish headed straight to the north and the other swimming on the horizon. The fish headed toward the north is the symbol of the aspirant to the mysteries while the fish on the horizon represents the average person.

The second constellation is Andromeda, the chained woman. We have three women among the constellations, Cassiopeia in Aries representing matter seated in her chair dominant; Coma Berenices in Virgo who sacrificed her hair to be of service, representing the soul only beginning to assert itself. Andromeda, the chained woman in Pisces represents matter harnessed.

The third constellation in Pisces is the King named Cepheus, the husband of Cassiopeia and the father of Andromeda. This suggests that "The King" represents the Spirit or Father aspect.

There is in nature the human kingdom and above it are other kingdoms, spiritual and cosmic, and below it there are the animal, vegetable and mineral kingdoms. The work of the intelligent sons of God is to act as transmitters, via the mind, of spiritual energy, which will save and vitalise all of nature.

The Second Coming of the Christ

How can the World Saviour come? He might come as he came before, in a physical body with its incidental handicaps. There are emerging in the world today new faculties that were not demonstrating when he came before. We are much more sensitive than we ever were; we are wide open to each other's thoughts for one thing, and if such a potent thinker as the Christ, whatever we may mean by that word, is en rapport with world affairs, it seems to me he might try another method. He may work with his own in every land, overshadowing his disciples wherever they are found, and because his soul and their souls are one, communicate to them the Plan, indicate to them the tendencies, give them the new message, and repeat himself in every country. It is already happening today. In every country there are to be found those who know; I did not say those who say they know. But there is a group of human beings, integrating now, who make no noise, are not interested in themselves, but upon whom is laid the burden of leading humanity. They are starting movements that have in them the new vibration, they are saying things that are universal in their tone, they are enunciating principles that are cosmic, they are inclusive and not exclusive, they do not care what terminology a man uses; they insist that a man shall keep his own inner structure of truth to himself and not impose it on any one else, they recognise each other wherever they meet, they speak a universal language, they demonstrate the universal light, they are servers and they have no interest in themselves.

I am convinced that no individual World Saviour, utilising a physical body, will come to us. I believe in that individual World Saviour, but I believe that he will save the world through the group. I believe that he will work through his own; that he raining people now so that the day will come when this group will be so potent through its silent meditation and the force of its world service, that it will be recognised as the Saviour; but not in our day.

Editor's Note:
When A.A.B. made this statement in 1936 it appears to have been the ashramic view that the status of humanity would not permit more than an overshadowing by the Christ. When *The Reappearance of the Christ*, dictated by the Tibetan, appeared in 1948, the discipline of the war, the destruction of material values, the suffering and the mental growth of humanity had produced an effect which we are told exceeded the expectations of the Hierarchy. In the book on the reappearance the following statements are found: "The point of decision, as it is called in all hierarchical circles, was reached during the period the Full Moon of June 1936 and the Full Moon of June 1945. The point of decision covered, therefore, nine years, a relatively brief time; it resulted in the decision arrived at by the Christ to appear or return to visible presence on Earth as soon as possible and considerably earlier than had been planned."

It is indeed a momentous thing to realise that humanity could so notably affect the time and manner of the reappearance of the Christ by a change in its receptivity. We have repeatedly been told that only humanity could condition these points. Here is a dramatic instance humanity's potential and responsibility in speeding up the evolutionary process.

The New Group of World Servers

Such a group as has just been described already exists. There are two things for us to do. First, to learn to recognize the new note as it comes from disciples wherever found and, secondly, fit ourselves to form part of that group. The hallmark of those people is not self-assertiveness; they are too busy doing salvage work to have time to talk about themselves. They work through meditation, which keeps them in touch with the spirituality that is themselves, and therefore is in touch with the Great Life, the World Saviour, who pours his force and energy through them and toward the world. They orient their minds in that direction, serve intelligently and are not in a hurry.

The message that comes to them from the inner side is couched in the symbolic words, "What I tell you in the dark, that speak you in the light." Each one will be told a different thing according to the need of the people around him, and will deliberately go into the dark in order to deliver a message in the light. Therefore, they are tied by no dogmas or doctrines because they have the word which has come to them in the dark, which they have wrought out for themselves in the strife and stress of their own souls. They meet the need of their fellow men, and theirs is the message of Christ, "A new commandment I give you that you love one another." This is no sentiment. Let us be loving and kind. That is just decent behaviour; but the love the Christ enunciated is an intelligent understanding and appreciation of the need of the individual just as you find him. When you are up against the desperate need of people you have no time to think about "being loving" in the usual sense. You can perhaps create such an atmosphere around yourself that they will think themselves through to their own solution. That is the real way to work. As long as you are occupied with being loving you are occupied with your own personality.

"A new commandment I give you" can be summed up in "inclusiveness", the hallmark of the New Age, the universal spirit, identification, oneness with all your fellowmen. That is love and it will keep you busy; you will have no time to talk about love, you will be busy doing things, big things and little things, unimportant and important things.

How shall we fit ourselves to meet that requirement, to possess those characteristics which automatically put us into the group of world servers? You will never get there by talking about it, or by theoretical appreciation of the problem. You will get there by doing the next thing correctly. That sounds very uninteresting, but whatever is your duty, do it. Cultivate the right inner attitude and be wide open to all your fellow men. Learn to meditate, and really learn to meditate. I am not talking of entering into the silence, of sitting down and having a blissful and peaceful time emoting, hoping that you will get up feeling better.

Meditation when rightly carried forward is hard mental work for it means orienting the mind to the soul, and you cannot do it. It means that when you have learned to focus your mind on the soul you must hold it steady, which you cannot do; and when you have learned to do that you must learn to listen in your mind to what the soul is telling you, and that you cannot do. Then you must learn to take what the soul has told you and form it into words and phrases and throw it down into your waiting brain. That is meditation, and it is by following that process that you will become a world server for you will then be the force of what you have accomplished. You will automatically find yourself overshadowed by that Great One whose mission it is to lift humanity out of darkness into light, from the unreal into the real.

Lecture by A.A.B.–1936. Edited and condensed.

THE PURPOSE OF THE STUDY OF THE HERCULES MYTH*

The first scriptures for the human race were written by God on the Earth and Heavens. The reading of these Scriptures is Science. Familiarity with the grass and trees, the insects and the infusoria, teaches us deeper lessons of love and faith than we can glean from the writings of Fénelon and Augustine. The great Bible of God is ever open before mankind.

–Albert Pike.

The heavens declare the glory of God; and the firmament sheweth his handywork.

–*Psalm* 19:1.

The progress of a world disciple is illustrated in the heavens by the Labours of Hercules through the zodiacal signs. It is as though God had pictured in space his Plan for the working out of the evolution of the human spirit back to its source.

* * *

The intense interest evinced at this time in the spiritual life is, in itself, the warrant for such a study as the Labours of Hercules. Academic, dogmatic and theological religion has no longer its ancient appeal but, in spite of a widespread revolt against organised, or ecclesiastical religion, the urge towards the spiritual realities has never been more keen than it is today. The period of empirical experience on a large scale is with us. Men and women everywhere are refusing any longer to believe the authoritative pronouncements of the churches or to accept blindly the dicta of any theology. They are determined to know for themselves the facts of the inner mystical experience, if such facts can be ascertained, and to grasp for themselves the nature of that identity which we call the soul.

---

*The following material was prepared by Dorothea Cochran at Mrs. Bailey's request and was found among her papers. This excerpt seems to provide an appropriate concluding note for the Hercules series.

The world setting is ripe for a renewal of a living faith and religion which will be based upon personal knowledge and not upon the pronouncements and the interpretations of limited minds. Dr. Rufus Jones, the great Quaker leader, calls attention to this fact in words which are worth noting:

" . . . an outbreak of mysticism is always a sign that the soul of man is uttering a vigorous protest against the encroachment of some organised system of life . . . which threatens to leave scant scope and area for its own free initiative and its spontaneous creative activity. It is a proclamation that the soul has certain inherent rights and capacities, a dominion of its own, which must be respected and held sacred. Sometimes mysticism has been the protest of man's spirit against the hardening crust of dogma, sometimes a revolt against ecclesiasticism."

The Philosophic Basis of Mysticism
by T.H. Hughes, page 46.

In days of darkness and apparent spiritual deadness, this revival of interest in the higher realities inevitably appears, guaranteeing that the spirit of man is on its way, and that the reality remains unchanged behind the changing surface of material events. The very need of the hour calls for the sounding of a clear note and to the newly emerging mystic and knower is given the task of this sounding. "What we find in the mystic is an intensified organ for the affirmation of the reality of God and for the richer interpretation of His character." With these clear words, Dr. Jones calls our attention to the work eternally done in the spiritual field by the awakened seeker.

Truth is, phoenix-like, emerging anew in the field of human experience, but it will be the truth which is felt and known and not the truth which is enforced through authoritarianism and ancient tradition; for truth, as Bernard Shaw tells us, is "what you know by your experience to be true and feel in your soul to be true". Such renewals of the spiritual life of the race are recurrent and cyclic; they can be of an emotional or an intellectual nature but they serve to lead the subjective life of the race into a new and richer phase of experience, and to offset, and sometimes to interpret, the more material and scientific paralleling trends which can be seen.

The problem of every writer and teacher today is to discover new ways in which to express the same foundational truths, and so to present the ancient formulas and rules of the road which will lead man to the next stage in his spiritual development. The old truths will then acquire new meanings and vibrate with fresh life. There have been many books written upon the subject of the Path of Discipleship. Restatement of the problems to be encountered upon the universal Path, and analysis of the difficulties to be faced whilst treading it is not warranted, unless the application can be general, practical and couched in such terms that meets the need of the modern student. A study of the Twelve Labours of Hercules, covering as they do every aspect of the disciple's life, may enable us to achieve a different attitude and release us into that joy on the Path and that freedom in service which is a more than adequate compensation for the temporary losses and momentary distresses which may try the lower nature.

One of the great revelations which has come almost unnoticed to humanity during the past century has been the slow dawning upon our consciousness of the fact of our own inherent essential divinity. Men are recognising that they are in very truth "made in the image of God", and are one in nature with their Father in Heaven. Today also, the purposes and plans underlying God's creative work are being studied widely from both the scientific and religious angles, bringing definite changes in man's attitude to life as a whole. It is this unfolding plan for man, individual and racial, that is revealed in the story of this ancient Son of God. We are given a synthetic and complete picture of the progress of the soul from ignorance to wisdom, from material desire to spirit aspiration, and from the blindness of infant humanity to the pure vision of those who see God. A point is reached in the story where intelligent cooperation with soul purpose takes the place of blind endeavour and struggle, and Hercules, who is a Son of God as well as a son of man, can proceed upon the *Way* with his face turned towards the light, irradiated by the joy of those who know.

This old tale leaves untouched no phases in the life of the aspirant and yet links him ceaselessly with cosmic enterprise. Its theme will be found to be so inclusive that all of us, immersed in the problems of life, can make application to ourselves of the tests and trials, the failures and achievements of this heroic figure, who strove, centuries ago, towards the same goal as we are striving. Through the reading of this story, fresh interest in the spiritual life may be evoked in the mind of the bewildered aspirant, and he will go forward with fresh courage as he gains a sequential picture of universal development and destiny.

We find, as we study this ancient myth that Hercules undertook certain tasks, symbolic in nature but universal in character, and that he passed through certain episodes and events which portray, for all time, the nature of the training and the attainments which should characterise a son of God, marching on towards perfection. He stands for the incarnated but not yet perfected Son of God, who, at a particular stage in the evolutionary cycle, takes his lower nature in hand and willingly subjects himself to the discipline which will eventually bring about the emergence of his innate divinity. Out of an erring but sincerely earnest human being, intelligently aware of the work to be done, a World Saviour is created, and we see in the last two labours how that work of saving was carried out.

Three great and dramatic stories have been told constantly to mankind down the ages: those of Hercules, the Buddha and the Christ, each of them portraying one of the stages upon the Path of Divinity. In the story of Hercules, we have portrayed for us the experiences of the Path of Discipleship and the early stages of the Path of Initiation. In the case of the Buddha, the story starts later than that of Hercules and we see the Buddha achieve final illumination, passing through initiations of which Hercules knew nothing. Then came the historic Christ, embodying in Himself something so ineffable that we regard Him, in a unique way, as the representative of God. These three stories progressively reveal God's plan for man's development, and call us to follow in the steps of Hercules, who trod the Path of Discipleship and attained his goal.

The oracle has spoken and down the centuries the cry has gone forth: "Know thyself." This knowledge is the outstanding attainment upon the Path of Discipleship, and it is seen how sequentially and intelligently Hercules attained this knowledge. We see him passing around the great pathway of the heavens and in each sign performing one of the twelve labours, which all disciples are called upon to perform. We see him from two viewpoints: that of the individual disciple and that of humanity as a whole, the great world disciple of which he is the prototype. It is possible to regard humanity as having reached, en masse, the stage of the aspirant, and to regard the race as standing upon the probationary path, the path of purification. If suffering is the great purifier; then the above statement is indeed true. Men today are intelligent, earnestly seeking a way out from the present material impasse and learning to co-ordinate their abilities and capacities, mental, emotional and physical, in an effort to rise above all that has hitherto held them down to earth. This stage has always been expressed by the more advanced types of men, but never before has the entire human family been in this condition. Herein lies the wonder of past achievement, and herein lies the hour of our wonderful opportunity.

We find Hercules starting at this point and passing through varying experiences until he comes to the open door in Leo, through which he can pass onto the Path of Discipleship. We see him learning the lessons of equilibrium, of selflessness and of victory over the desire nature until he becomes the one-pointed disciple in Sagittarius, prior to passing through the gate which leads to the mount of initiation. Slowly and painfully, he learns the lesson that competition and selfish grasping must disappear and that the seizing of anything for the separated lower self is no part of the mission of a son of God. He finds himself as an individual only to discover that individualism must be intelligently sacrificed to the good of the group; he learns that personal greed has no place in the life of the aspirant who is seeking liberation from the ever recurring cycle of existence and constant crucifixion upon the cross of matter and form. The characteristics of the man immersed in form life and under the rule of matter are fear, individual competition and greed. These have to give place to spiritual confidence, cooperation, group awareness and selflessness. These are the lessons which Hercules brings to us.

This is also the story of the cosmic Christ, crucified from the beginning of creation upon the fixed cross of the heavens. This is the story of the historical Christ, given us in the gospel story and enacted for us two thousand years ago in Palestine, when our sun entered the sign of the world Saviour, the sign of Pisces, the fishes. This is the story of every individual man, crucified upon the cross of matter and of existence, and discovering that he is in truth a son of God incarnated in each human being. God, incarnate in matter. Such is the story of the solar system, the story of our planet, the story of every man. As we look at the starry heavens above us, we have this great drama, eternally pictured for us.

SUMMARY OF LESSONS LEARNED IN EACH ZODIACAL SIGN

The following abstract of notes on the zodiacal signs is offered as a basis for further study and quick reference.

Aries, the Ram

Element: Fire sign (as are also Leo and Sagittarius).

Quality: Initiating. Beginnings. Will or Power expresses itself through the great creative processes. In the early stages, activities are directed toward the material side of life; later, toward the spiritual.

Polar Opposite: Libra. An air sign (balance).

Rulers: Exoteric, Mars; Esoteric, Mercury.

Keywords: From the angle of form, "Let form again be sought"; from the angle of soul, "I come forth and from the plane of mind, I rule".

Taurus, the Bull

Element: Earth sign (as are also Virgo and Capricorn).

Quality: Desire, for the mass of men; will or directed purpose for the disciple.

Polar Opposite: Scorpio, water sign (conflict of duality, desire overcome; triumphant discipleship).

Rulers: Exoteric, Venus; Esoteric, Vulcan.

Keywords: From the angle of form, "Let struggle be undismayed"; from the angle of soul, "I see and when the Eye is opened, all is illumined".

Gemini, the Twins

Element: Air sign (as are also Libra and Aquarius).

Quality: Duality. Love-Wisdom. Fluidity. Control of every pair of opposites. The underlying love of Deity reaches our solar system through Gemini.

Polar Opposite: Sagittarius. A fire sign (one-pointedness; preparation for initiation).

Rulers: Exoteric, Mercury; Esoteric, Venus.

Keywords: From the angle of form, "Let instability do its work"; from the angle of soul, "I recognise my other self and in the waning of that self I grow and glow."

Cancer, the Crab

Element: Water sign (as are also Scorpio and Pisces).

Quality: Mass sensitivity; for the average man, mass identification with form; for the disciple, service for the masses.

Polar Opposite: Capricorn. An earth sign (spiritual awareness after struggle; birthplace of the Christ).

Rulers: Exoteric, the Moon; Esoteric, Neptune.

Keywords: From the angle of form, "Let isolation be the rule, and yet the crowd exists;" from the angle of soul, "I build a lighted house and therein dwell".

Leo, the Lion

Element: Fire sign (as are also Aries and Sagittarius).

Quality: Sensitivity leading to individual awareness. Emergence out of the herd. Self-consciousness. Self assertion.

Polar Opposite: Aquarius. An air sign (group awareness, world service).

Rulers: Exoteric and Esoteric are the same, the Sun.

Keywords: From the angle of form, "Let other forms exist, I am because I am," from the angle of soul, "I am That and That am I."

Virgo, the Virgin

Element: Earth sign (as are also Taurus and Capricorn).

Quality: The unique service in Virgo is that both the form and the spirit are nurtured, shielding "Christ in you the hope of glory"

Polar Opposite: Pisces. A water sign (Christ consciousness revealed as a World Saviour).

Rulers: Exoteric, Mercury; Esoteric, the Moon.

Keywords: From the angle of form, "Let matter reign"; from the angle of soul, "I am the Mother and the Child. I, God, I, matter am".

Libra, the Balance

Element: Air sign (as are also Gemini and Aquarius).

Quality: Equilibrium. An interlude where duality is known and the life of soul and form is balanced (Law, Sex, Money).

Polar Opposite: Aries. A fire sign (subjective, latent consciousness, will to incarnate).

Rulers: Exoteric, Venus; Esoteric, Uranus.

Keywords: From the angle of form, "Let choice be made"; from the angle of soul, "I choose the way which leads between the two great lines of force."

Scorpio, the Scorpion

Element: Water sign (as are also Cancer and Pisces).

Quality: Conflict. Test. Trial. Triumph. Points of crisis. Moments of re-orientation. Turning point in the life of humanity and of the individual. Hercules became the triumphant disciple in Scorpio.

Polar Opposite: Taurus. An earth sign (desire, and growth of soul light).

Rulers: Exoteric and Esoteric, the same, Mars.

Keywords: From the angle of form, "Let Maya flourish and let deception rule"; from the angle of soul, "Warrior I am and from the battle I emerge triumphant".

Sagittarius, the Archer

Element: Fire sign (as are also Aries and Leo).

Quality: Focussed direction. One-pointed activity. In the early stages, satisfaction of desire; in later stages aspiration for the goal of initiation.

Polar Opposite: Gemini. An air sign (eventual control of fluidity and pairs of opposites; fusion, synthesis, at-one-ment).

Rulers: Exoteric, Jupiter; Esoteric, Earth.

Keywords: From the angle of form, "Let food be sought"; from the angle of soul, "I see the goal. I reach that goal and then I see another".

Capricorn, the Goat

Element: Earth sign (as are also Taurus and Virgo).

Quality: Extreme characteristics of the worst and best types. Ambition. Crystallisation. Struggle overcome. Transfiguration. Initiate consciousness. "The unicorn of God."

Polar Opposite: Cancer. A water sign (first door to incarnation).

Rulers: Exoteric and Esoteric the same, Saturn.

Keywords: From the angle of form, "Let ambition rule and let the door stand wide;" from the angle of soul, "Lost am I in light supernal, yet on that light I turn my back".

Aquarius, the Water Carrier

Element: Air sign (as are also Gemini and Libra).

Quality: Will to serve, first the lower self, then the higher Self. World service. Individual consciousness transmuted into group consciousness.

Polar Opposite: Leo, A fire sign (individual awareness; urge toward self-knowledge; eventual self-mastery preparatory to selfless service).

Rulers: Exoteric, Uranus; Esoteric, Jupiter.

Keywords: From the angle of form, "Let desire in form be the rule"; from the angle of soul, "Water of Life am I, poured forth for thirsty men".

Pisces, the Fishes

Element: Water sign (as are also Cancer and Scorpio).

Quality: Duality. Fluidity endowed with instinctual consciousness. Mediumistic. Polarised mind unawakened. Intuition dormant. Death of the personality. Release of the soul from captivity. Christ, the World Saviour.

Polar Opposite: Virgo. An earth sign (matter; Christ in the cave of the heart).

Rulers: Exoteric, Jupiter; Esoteric, Pluto.

Keywords: From the angle of form, "Go forth into matter"; from the angle of soul, "I leave my Father's home and turning back, I save".

THE PATH OF THE SOUL THROUGH THE ZODIAC

"The path of souls to ascension lies through the twelve signs of the Zodiac...the descending path is the same."

CLEMENT OF ALEXANDRIA.

Editor's Note: Lest we be lost in the colourful labours of Hercules, and the marvels of this allegory of the labours of all disciples on their evolutionary way, or be confined to the personal correlation with our own sun sign in this one incarnation, it seems wise to turn our thoughts to the deeper significance of the energies of these signs which fall upon our little planet, and the use we make of them. The larger picture of the effect on world and racial evolution should receive our thought. The Tibetan tells us that all depends upon our degree of receptivity and response, which is determined by our status of evolution.

In the life of Hercules, the soul in incarnation, and his progress round the Zodiac from Aries to Pisces on the reversed wheel, the path of the disciple, it might be helpful to briefly define the Zodiac so that we can follow his labours intelligently. It might also be of benefit to ascertain whether; in our western Christian tradition, there are indications of the influence of the ancient science of astrology.

There have been many definitions of the word "Zodiac." The most usual is as follows:

" . . . the word is derived from the Greek 'zodion', a little animal, full expression being the zodiacal circle, or circle of animals. This was an imaginary belt in the sky, formed by two circles equidistant from the ecliptic and about eighteen degrees apart, which marked out the path of the sun either in its annual revolution when the twelve divisions indicated the succession of months in the year; or in its diurnal course, when the divisions marked the hours of the day and night."

Astrology, the Link between Two Worlds.
by S. Elizabeth Hall, M.A.

Valentia Stratton might also be quoted here:

" . . . in astronomy, says science, the Zodiac is an imaginary belt in the heavens, sixteen or eighteen degrees broad, through the middle of which passes the sun's path (the ecliptic). It contains the twelve constellations, which constitute the twelve signs of the Zodiac, and from which they are named. . . . The astrological Zodiac proper; however, is an imaginary circle passing around the earth in the plane of the ecliptic, its first point being called Aries, 0 degrees. It is divided into twelve equal parts called 'signs of the Zodiac', each containing thirty degrees of space, and on it is measured the right ascension of the celestial bodies. The movable or natural Zodiac is a succession of constellations forming a belt of 47 degrees in width, lying north and south of the ecliptic."

Glossary of *The Celestial Ship of the North.*

Walter H. Samson gives us a very simple explanation of the imaginary belt. He says:

"The Zodiac, properly speaking, is that belt of the heavens through which passes the apparent path of the sun; its point of commencement is the Vernal Equinox which, as we know, is in continuous retrograde movement through a circle of constellations which lie near the ecliptic. The Zodiac is divided into twelve equal portions of thirty degrees each, corresponding loosely to the twelve constellations of Aries, Taurus, Gemini, Cancer, Leo, Virgo, Libra, Scorpio, Sagittarius, Capricorn, Aquarius and Pisces."

The Zodiac: A Life Epitome.

Alan Leo tells us also:

"...the constellations are groups of fixed stars, the twelve central groups being called by the same names as the twelve signs, although they do not cover the same area of the heavens. The precession of the equinoxes, caused by the 'motion' of the sun through space, makes the constellations appear to move forward against the order of the signs at the rate of 50 1/3rd seconds per year."   *Dictionary of Astrology*, p. 204.

Another point to be remembered is made by Alan Leo in the following:

"The twelve constellations form the Zodiac of the whole solar system. . . just as the rotation of the earth makes the signs rise and set, a new sign being on the ascendant every two hours on an average; so, as the result of the precession, the far greater circle of the constellations passes across the earth's ascendant, the equinoctial point, the beginning of the Zodiac. In this way, the great day of precession, comprising over twenty-five thousand of our years, corresponds with one of our days, because during that period all the twelve constellations rise and set once."

Ibid, p. 167

The second thing, therefore, to remember is that there are two Zodiacs, the greater and the lesser. The former comprises the twelve constellations through which the sun and planetary system appear to pass in a great cycle of over 25,000 years. The latter is the same circle of constellations through which the earth appears to pass in its annual revolution around the sun, and it is upon this that the astrologers base their predictions and cast the horoscope. Thus we have in these two Zodiacs the symbol of the progress of the Life informing a solar system, a planet and a man.

"As the earth in its yearly journey around the sun passes through a sign of the Zodiac each month, so does our solar system during its great journey around the central sun of the universe (Alcyone) pass through each sign of the Zodiac; but in this greater cycle instead of a month our solar system requires approximately two thousand and sixty years to traverse each sign."

The Message of Aquaria, p. 23, by Homer Curtiss.

An interesting and more probable definition of the word "Zodiac" is given by Dr. Ethelbert Bullinger in his book *The Witness of the Stars*. He says:

"The word Zodiac itself is from the Greek 'Zodiakon', which is not from 'zoon' 'to live', but from a primitive root, through the Hebrew 'sodi', which in Sanskrit means 'a way'. Its etymology has no connection with living creatures, but denotes a way, or steps and is used for the way or path which the sun appears to follow amongst the stars in the course of a year."

The Zodiac, therefore, is the Path or Way. When Christ spoke to His disciples as the Cosmic Christ, He told them "I am the Way", and to this it is possible to give an astrological significance, for all three types of lives tread this cosmic Way, the Cosmic Christ, the Planetary Spirit and the human being.

It is interesting to note that the Zodiac is spoken of as an illusion and as an imaginary path, an appearance. Webster's Dictionary, for instance, defines the Zodiac as "the imaginary path of the sun through the heavens", and in all books of reference upon the subject the emphasis is laid upon the fact that it is all appearance, the great illusion. One writer tells us that:

". . . to the astronomer the Zodiac is merely the pathway of the sun, the moon and the planets, possessing no more reality than the tracks of liners shown upon an atlas for the information of the intending travellers."

The Zodiac and the Soul, p.l,
by C.E.O. Carter

As we study this imaginary path two thoughts emerge. We are brought face to face with the concept of a steady and unceasing progression around and around this vast belt of constellations. The idea of eternal recurrence and of constant activity, bringing with it, we hope and believe, a constant development, gives us a grasp of the magnitude of the One Life and a vision of an ever-emerging plan and purpose, which embodies the intelligent working out of God's thought.

The second idea, which found such a strong response in the human mind that it constitutes what is called "the science of astrology" and forms its basic premise, is that each of these signs, through which the sun and earth appear to pass, are embodiments of energies which have a potent effect upon all forms of life on our planet, and upon the world of ideas. Humanity, it is contended, has been and is affected by energies contacted by our solar system as it passes in and out of the various constellations. If this is a fact, and if we can get a wide enough retrospect, it should surely be possible to demonstrate the truth of this contention.

How then can these energies be effective? It is said that it is through the thought form that they are transmitted. We glibly use the phrase, "energy follows thought". Here the reality of this belief is put to a cosmic test. Death is also said to be "a figment of our imagination".

Testimony as to the Effectiveness of Zodiacal Energies on Earth Life:

In the larger picture certain interesting facts emerge. We can say, for instance, that between four and five thousand years ago the sun was somewhere in the sign Taurus, the Bull. Then we had the worship of the bull in Egypt and in India, and the sacrifice of the sacred ox, as in the Mysteries of Mithras.

Approximately two thousand years before the birth of Christ, astronomers tell us, the sun passed into the sign Aries, the Ram or Lamb, and the Jewish dispensation came into being. At that time, therefore, we have the inauguration of the Jewish Passover and the lamb sacrifice. It is interesting to note in this connection the true significance of the sin of the Children of Israel in the wilderness. We read that they made a golden calf and fell down and worshipped it, thus reverting in this act to ancient forms and sacrifices. Their sin consisted in a reactionary attitude and in not grasping the significance of the new age which was upon them.

Again the astronomers tell us that, when Christ was born in Palestine, the date from which our Christian dispensation starts, the sun passed in to the sign Pisces, the Fishes. We have, therefore, the emphasis laid in the Gospel story upon the fish symbology. Christ chose fishermen to be among His disciples; He performed miracles with fishes; He sent His disciples out into the world to be fishers of men; for nearly two thousand years it has been customary to eat fish on Good Friday and on fast days. So we find the lamb sacrifice following upon the bull sacrifice, and the fish symbol upon that of the lamb, and this as the sun passed apparently from Taurus into Aries and from Aries into Pisces.

Now we are passing into the sign Aquarius, the water carrier, though we have not yet entered fully into that sign, a process that will take approximately a further two hundred years. We are informed by the astronomers that we began to transit into that sign about two hundred years ago, and it is discernible how, since then, Aquarius, the water carrier; has begun to make his presence felt in the development of sanitation and the prolific use of water. But Aquarius is an air sign and the skies are full of aircraft. Even, therefore, in its exoteric forms, the influence of the signs is surely substantiated and there is a real foundation for the claim of the esotericist that each new sign brings to the earth distinctive energies, new concepts and new opportunities.

It can also be shown that these astrological factors have set their mark upon our Christian tradition and upon our Church usage. It is interesting to note in this connection that on Christmas Eve, the brightest of the fixed stars, Sirius, is seen to the left of the meridian line somewhat to the south. Two thousand years ago, owing to the precession of the equinoxes, it stood on the meridian line. This is the Star in the East. At the same time, the constellation Virgo, the Virgin, became visible in the east, and it is interesting to note the co-incidence that Spica, the brightest star in that constellation, means "an ear of wheat," and Bethlehem, the town in which Christ was born, means "the house of bread." When this arrangement cyclically comes about in the heavens, the great historic Sons of God make their appearance for the uplift of humanity and the saving of the world. It is also said that the conjunction of Saturn and Jupiter created a brilliant, arresting appearance.

One other instance of the effect of the constellations upon our Christian faith might be given. Two festivals are kept in the Roman Catholic and the Anglican Churches, called the Assumption of the Virgin, celebrated on August 15th, and the Birth of the Virgin on September 8th. Each year the sun enters the sign Virgo around August 15th and the stars of which it is composed are lost sight of in the glory of the sun's rays. At the time of the ancient picturing of the Zodiac, August 15th would see the actual disappearance of the cluster Virgo, but now the time is not exact, though the Church perpetuates the original date. On or about September 8th the constellation can be seen from our planet slowly emerging from out of the rays of the sun and reappearing. This we speak of as the birth of the Virgin.

Two other indications can be given to show how widely and deeply the Zodiac has affected our religious beliefs. One will be seen as we study the significance of the Twelve Sons of Jacob and the pronouncements made by their father; and the other emerges as we study the origin of the Cross.

The Crosses:

The subject of the Cross is too vast a one to be elucidated here. The cross within the circle is one of be most ancient of the world's symbols, antedating the Christian era by thousands of years. The cross is originally formed by the interplay between the twelve signs of the Zodiac. There are in the Zodiac thirty-six crosses, for each sign is divided into what are called three decanates, which used to be known as "the thirty-six crossing stars." The Zodiac is completed with 360 degrees, the square of 90 degrees is one fourth of the circle, creating the four corners, which is the cross within the circle.

There are, however; three main crosses which in their symbology represent the three divine aspects, Spirit, Soul and Body. They are as follows:

1. The Cardinal Cross, consisting of the four constellations:
   - a. Aries . . . .   Creation, commencement.
   - b. Cancer . . . . .   The first door into existence.
   - c. Libra . . . .   The balance between life and form.
   - d. Capricorn . . .   The door into spiritual life.

This is the cross of Spirit or of the initiate and it is interesting to note that the word "cardinal" comes from a Latin word meaning "the hinge of a door." The word "door" enters much into the concept of discipleship and it implies the period preparatory to passing through the door or gate of initiation. Here we have the idea of the door through which the Cosmic Christ passes at the end of the age when the heavens and the earth are dissolved and God's plans are consummated.

2. The Fixed Cross, consisting of the four constellations:
   - a. Taurus . . . . . .   Illumination. Mind.
   - b. Leo . . . .   Individuality. Self-consciousness.
   - c. Scorpio . . . . .   The final freeing from illusion.
   - d. Aquarius . . . .   Server of the race, pouring out the living water of purification.

This is pre-eminently the cross of the soul and of real interest because it is the cross of the disciple Hercules. He personified these four signs, and was crucified upon this Fixed Cross. These four signs are regarded in our Christian belief as the Sacred Four and we find them presented to us in the four living creatures of the prophet Ezekiel. These four had the face of a man, Aquarius; the face of a lion, Leo; the face of an ox, Taurus; and the face of an eagle, Scorpio. Aquila, the Eagle is astrologically interchangeable with Scorpio. They are symbolised again in the four evangelists, and in the four beasts of Revelations. This cross is the cross of all world saviours, and the cardinal cross is that of Deity, crucified in the water of space.

3. The Mutable or Common Cross, consisting of the four constellations:

a. Gemini. . . . . The interplay between higher and lower.

b. Virgo . . . . . . The form which nurtures the Christ child.

c. Sagittarius . . The Aspirant, speeding towards the goal.

d. Pisces . . . . . Death. Consummation. The World Saviour.

This is the cross of everyday life to which all the sons of men are subjected. It is the cross of daily crucifixion and of difficulty and symbolises the incarnation period of growth and development through the medium of form and its use. In these three crosses is summed up the story of the Cosmic Christ, God crucified in matter, of Hercules and of all disciples, and of the average human being. They constitute the totality of the twelve signs.

The Sign	*Son of Jacob*	*Remarks*
Aries. The Ram, Lamb	Naphtali.	Naphtali is a play upon the Hebrew word "taleh", the Ram. It means the twisting and struggling ram. Note the story of Abraham and the ram caught in the thicket.
Taurus. The Bull.	Issachar.	"He bowed his shoulders to bear." This refers to the yoke and the work of the ox in producing crops.
Gemini. The Twins	Simeon and Levi.	"Simeon and Levi are brothers"
Cancer. The Crab.	Zebulon.	He "wished for habitation, dwelling at the haven of the sea". The crab carries its habitation on its back, and dwells on the sea shore.
Leo. The Lion.	Judah.	Judah is a lion's whelp. "He couched as a lion."
Virgo. The Virgin.	Asher.	This name is from Ishtar. Ashera is the goddess of plenty. She is depicted as a virgin, carrying a sheaf of wheat. See Gen. 49, 20.

The Sign	*Son of Jacob*	*Remarks*
Libra. The Scales or Balances.	Dan.	"Dan shall judge his people."
Scorpio. The Serpent or Adder.	Dan.	Mentioned twice as two sons are assigned to Gemini. "Dan shall be a serpent . . . that biteth the horses' heels."
Sagittarius.	Joseph.	"His bow abode in strength". His horse is the one that Scorpio follows fast after.
Capricorn. The Goat	Benjamin.	In the Egyptian mysteries Capricorn is represented as a God with a wolf's head. "Benjamin shall raven as a wolf."
Aquarius. The Water Carrier	Reuben.	Means "the pouring out of water." The living water.
Pisces. The Fishes.	Gad.	A play on "Dag", the fish.

JOURNEY THROUGH THE SIGNS

(As a back-drop to the drama enacted in each Sign this brief summary seems to integrate the Hercules Series)

The progress of Hercules from the mental plane, through the emotional or desire plane and out into physical manifestation, and then his journey through the twelve signs, and by means of the twelve labours, to the point where he becomes an inspired Initiate, can be outlined for us briefly in the following statement:

In *Aries* (March 21-April 20*, the Ram), through the capture of the Man-Eating Mares, we see him make his start, react to thought impulse, and learn something of mind control. As the intelligent disciple, he starts out upon his career; beginning with an undefined spiritual urge to righteousness and ending as the world saviour.

In *Taurus* (April 21-May 20, the Bull), he has to learn the nature of desire, to transmute it into aspiration, to dominate sex, and use it rightly, and thus capture the Cretan Bull. This strong urge, and the potency of attraction, is that, as we shall see, which produces the great illusion, but which can, eventually, become the cause of illumination.

Passing on into the sign *Gemini* (May 21-June 20, the Twins), the progress of the disciple, hitherto subjective and characterised by thought and desire, works out into expression on the physical plane. In this sign he arrives at knowledge of himself as a personality and gathers the golden apples of knowledge, subordinating to his enterprise the three aspects of the personal lower self, the physical body, the desire-feeling nature and the mind.

In *Cancer* (June 21-July 21, the Crab), the higher faculty of the intuition is brought into play, and this is symbolised for

---

* The dates given are approximate, they vary according to different authorities.

us in the capture of the elusive Doe, or Hind, sensitive and difficult to find. In his previous cycles of life experience, he has transmuted instinct into intellect, but now as the disciple, he must transmute intellect into intuition. The higher correspondences of all the lower powers have to be developed and utilised.

Thus equipped, in *Leo* (July 22-August 21, the Lion), he undertakes the best known of his labours, the killing of the Nemean Lion. He demonstrates in this test the power to do two things and proves to his watching master, Eurystheus, that his refocussed and coordinated personality is characterised by that determined courage which is the gift of people born in this sign, and he testifies through this labour also that the lower can be subordinated to the higher. Through the service rendered and the sanity of his procedure he gives a guarantee of the strength of his purpose.

We might regard these five labours in Aries, Taurus, Gemini, Cancer and Leo, as covering the entire period of the Path of Probation, and the killing of the Nemean Lion is the climax of that part of the struggle. Now he is ready to tread the Path of Discipleship, in which the indwelling Christ is gradually revealed, matter is steadily subordinated to the uses of the soul, and the form aspect comes to be regarded simply as the mother of the Christ Child. This progressive knowledge begins in Virgo, the sixth sign, the sign of the manger; and is consummated in Capricorn, the tenth sign, the birth sign of all the sun gods. On the Path of Discipleship, he has, secondly, to demonstrate that he has overcome illusion, that the magical glamour that matter imposes upon spirit no longer deludes. This is dramatically shown in the labour performed in Scorpio, the killing of the Nine-Headed Hydra. After Capricorn, he becomes a server of humanity, consecrated to the work of the Hierarchy, and this spiritual dedication to service finds its expression in the two last signs of the zodiacal round, those of Aquarius and Pisces.

In *Virgo* (August 22-September 21, the Virgin), therefore, the first of the disciple signs, he performs his sixth labour; and seizes the girdle of Hippolyte, the Queen of the Amazons. It is interesting to note that the first labour on the probationary path started with a partial failure, in Aries, and the first labour on the Path of Discipleship in Virgo is also "done, but badly done". The disciple must never be off his guard, for there is always the danger of error and of mistake. His very virtues can become his problem and we are told that it is possible even for a high initiate son of God to drop back from the Path of Attainment. His failure is, however; only temporary. Fresh opportunities occur. The consequence of his mistake has been delay, but the day of restoration and of renewal inevitably recurs. In Virgo we have depicted the preparation for the first initiation, the birth of the Christ, called in Christianity the birth of the Christ in the heart. This is a physical plane happening as well as a transcendental one, as we find when we study the signs of Virgo and of Capricorn.

In *Libra* (September 22-October 21, the Balance), Hercules captures the Boar and, through the performance of this labour, demonstrates his fitness to take the second initiation, which concerns the emotional body. He balances the pairs of opposites and demonstrates it in an amusing and symbolic manner. He proves that poise and equilibrium are now achieved characteristics and that he is fit to undertake the tremendous task provided for him in the next sign.

In *Scorpio* (October 23-November 22, the Scorpion), he enters upon his supreme test, which is also the supreme test for humanity, and which, if we study the times and seasons, appears that to which humanity is subjected at the present time. The problem before Hercules was his emancipation from illusion and the freeing of perception from the mists and miasmas, the glamour and the appearances, behind which Reality veils itself. In this sign he passes successfully through his greatest trial and thenceforth his problem changes. He has controlled and demonstrated his capacity to overcome desire; he is poised and balanced in his point of view; now, because he is no longer taken in by that which appears and because he can walk one-pointedly in the Light, he becomes a world worker.

This one-pointedness is demonstrated for us in *Sagittarius* (November 23-December 22, the Archer), where we have the consummation of the task begun in Aries, which was the right use and control of thought. In Aries he captured the Man-Eating Mares and bent them to his use. Now he slays the Man-Eating Birds of Stymphalos and puts an end to all tendencies to use thought destructively.

In *Capricorn* (December 23-January 20, the Goat), he becomes an initiate and appears before the world as a saviour; a liberated son of God, able to work in Hell, on Earth, or in Heaven. He carries Cerberus up from Hades, and through the symolism of the three-headed dog portrays the elevation of the personality, the triple matter aspect, into Heaven. Thus he demonstrates that he has undergone the necessary development and experienced the strengthening tests which will enable him successfully to pass through the experience of the third initiation, that of the Transfiguration.

The next two signs, Aquarius and Pisces, show us the liberated Hercules at his work, the saving of the world. His tests are no longer personal and individual, but are universal in their application and demonstrate to us the inclusiveness of the consciousness and the vastness of the methods employed by the disciple who has climbed the mountain in Capricorn and has no longer any personal problems.

In *Aquarius* (January 21-February 19, the Water Carrier), Hercules cleaned the Augean Stables by turning a river through them. They had not been cleaned for many years. Thus did he symbolically pour out the cleansing waters in service to man. This is the important sign into which we are now entering; the most menial of all the labours falls in this, next to the culminating labour of all. One may think with reverence of Jesus the Christ washing the feet of his disciples, after following the man with the water pitcher on his shoulder; into the upper room.

In *Pisces* (February 20-March 20, the Fishes), we find by contrast the most exalted symbol. For here Hercules captured the Red Cattle, placed them in a golden bowl (the Holy Grail), and flew them to the Temple. Such is the crowning beauty of the sign in which man becomes a world saviour, all that is of animality having been redeemed and transcended. *Interpolated.*

This short analysis of the twelve labours will give us a somewhat synthetic picture of the work done by every disciple who is truly in earnest, as he progresses from Aries to Pisces. It is a work arduous, slow and carried forward under great difficulties, and often in blind ignorance of the forces released and of the results to be achieved. But step by step the aspirant is led along the path of self-knowledge. His character and nature have been tested and tried until the qualities which characterise the form have been transmuted into those which reveal the soul.

* * *

"The help has to come from a source other than this limited existence, but this source must not be something wholly outside us, in the sense that it has no understanding of our limitations, and hence is not in any way sympathetic with us. The source of help must have the same heart as ours so that there will be a current of compassion running between the two. The source-power must be within us and yet outside. If not within us, it could not understand us; if not outside, it would be subject to the same conditions. This is an eternal problem, to be and not to be, to be within and yet to be outside, to be finite and yet ready to serve the infinite."

D. T. Suzuki.

ARCANE SCHOOL TRAINING

Training for new age discipleship is provided

by the *Arcane School.* The principles of the

Ageless Wisdom are presented through esoteric

meditation, study and service as a *way of life.*

****

www.lucistrust.org/arcaneschool